Stefan Buczacki's
Gardening Britain

Stefan
Buczacki's

GARDENING
BRITAIN

AN ESSENTIAL GUIDE
FOR GARDEN LOVERS
EVERYWHERE

BBC BOOKS

This book is published to
accompany the television series entitled
Stefan Buczacki's Gardening Britain which
was first broadcast in November 1996
EXECUTIVE PRODUCER Clare Stride
SERIES PRODUCER Claire Boulter

Published by BBC Books,
an imprint of BBC Worldwide Publishing.
BBC Worldwide Limited, Woodlands,
80 Wood Lane, London W12 0TT

ISBN 0 563 38787 4

Edited and designed for BBC Books
by Brown Packaging Books Ltd
DESIGNER Rosamund Saunders
EDITOR Barbara Segall
MAPS Stephen Dew

Printed in Great Britain by Cambus Litho Ltd, East Kilbride
Bound in Great Britain by Hunter & Foulis Ltd, Edinburgh
Jacket printed by Lawrence Allen Ltd, Weston-super-Mare

CONTENTS

GARDENING BRITAIN

These maps show the range
of rainfall in Britain and the
areas with predominantly
acid or alkaline soils. In
combination, they give rise
to the great variety of
gardening environments on
these islands.

The map on this page
also shows the locations of
the gardens featured in
the book.

SOIL TYPES

acid

alkaline

PITMEDDEN
CRATHES CASTLE

MEGGINCH
CASTLE

HODNET HALL

BLICKLING HALL

BURFORD HOUSE
HERGEST
CROFT

ICKWORTH

HELMINGHAM HALL

WESTONBIRT

HESTERCOMBE
KNIGHTSHAYES
COURT

HILLIER
ARBORETUM

NATIONAL
PINETUM

MOUNT EDGCUMBE

TREWITHEN
TREBAH

ATHELHAMPTON

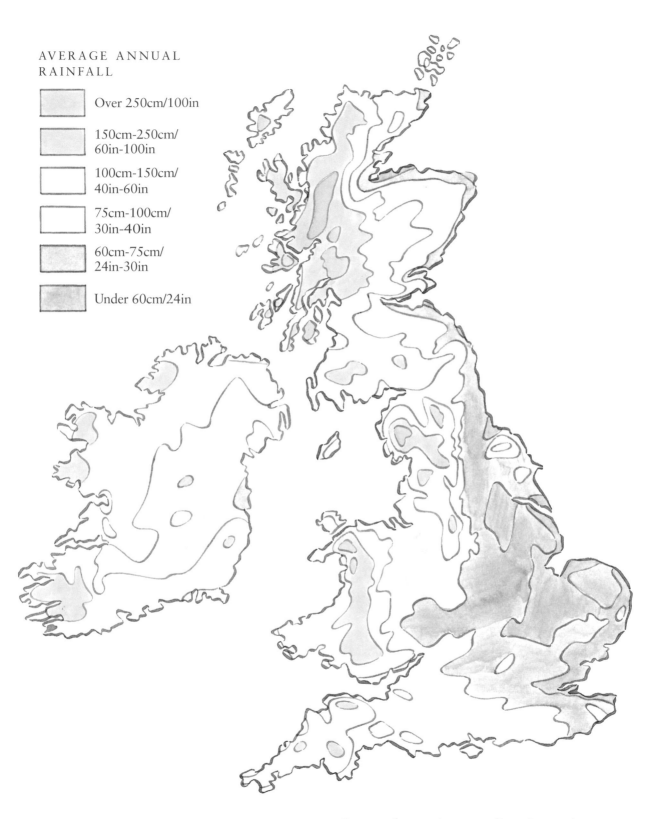

AVERAGE ANNUAL
RAINFALL

Over 250cm/100in

150cm-250cm/
60in-100in

100cm-150cm/
40in-60in

75cm-100cm/
30in-40in

60cm-75cm/
24in-30in

Under 60cm/24in

Gardening Britain 7

INTRODUCTION

AS GARDENERS, the British need feel envy for no-one. Within the confines of our small islands we have the finest and most varied gardening environment in the world. Of course, there are consistently warmer places, although reliably warm or hot summers are commonly accompanied by extreme dryness and followed by reliably cold winters. Our climate by contrast is equable; it lacks those extremes of heat and cold. And whilst there may indeed be places with an equally equable environment, none can compete with us for variety. The variety, however, comes not from climate but from geology. I don't think there are any areas of comparable size to Britain with so great a range of rock types, and these in turn have resulted in a great many different soils.

But as I say several times during the programmes, gardening is as much about people as the environment. Every garden is the result of someone's likes and dislikes, successes and failures. It's an extension of one individual's personality. And here too, we have been doubly blessed. First we have produced some astonishingly adventurous and courageous plant collectors and explorers. Men have left Britain to visit the furthest and most inaccessible reaches of the planet where they have garnered a rich harvest of seeds and plants to bring home. Our second blessing has been our ability to generate fine and talented horticulturists. It is indeed one thing to have the environment, and another to have the plants. To be able to take those raw materials and create the fine-art that results in great gardens is a rare ability. That a number of pivotal figures in gardening history have so demonstrably achieved this is, I'm sure, the reason that today there is such a depth and breadth of gardening ability encompassing all regions of the country and all strata of society.

In *Gardening Britain* I've visited some fine and glorious gardens and met the people who have created them or who have used them in turn, to derive the inspiration for another creativity. Although I visited several different regions, the questions and problems I encountered are relevant to gardens all over the country. Each

GARDENS

FEATURED

ATHELHAMPTON HOUSE & GARDENS
Dorset
Tel: 01305 848363

BLICKLING HALL
Norfolk
Tel: 01263 733471

BURFORD HOUSE
Shropshire
Tel: 01584 810777

CRATHES CASTLE
Aberdeenshire
Tel: 01330 844525

HELMINGHAM HALL
Suffolk
Tel: 01473 890363

HERGEST CROFT GARDENS
Herefordshire
Tel: 01544 230160

HESTERCOMBE
Somerset
Tel: 01823 337222

HODNET HALL
Shropshire
Tel: 01630 685202

ICKWORTH HOUSE
Suffolk
Tel: 01284 735270

KNIGHTSHAYES
GARDENS
Devon
Tel: 01884 254665

MEGGINCH
CASTLE
Perthshire
Tel: 01821 642222

MOUNT
EDGCUMBE
Cornwall
Tel: 01752 822236

NATIONAL
PINETUM
Bedgebury,
Kent
Tel: 01580 211044

PITMEDDEN
Aberdeenshire
Tel: 01651 842352

SIR HAROLD
HILLIER
ARBORETUM
Hampshire
Tel: 01794 368787

TREBAH
Cornwall
Tel: 01326 250448

TREWITHEN
Cornwall
Tel: 01726 882763

WESTONBIRT
GARDENS
Gloucestershire
Tel: 01666 880233

See also map on page 6

chapter outlines some of the characteristics of each area, but with the emphasis on the similarities we all share. Many of the questions I was asked are included, together with the answers I gave. For gardens may be personal creations but gardening itself is very much a shared experience. I've met countless fellow gardeners thirsting for knowledge and information. And whilst there is undoubtedly a hard core of questions that crop up with predictable regularity, every meeting with new gardening friends results in something different.

I consider myself fortunate in having spent years of my professional life engaged in scientific research, and working in a field that gives rise to more gardening questions than almost any other. For I was involved with research in Plant Pathology; into the causes, biology and cures of plant afflictions. I would guess that these comprise at least half of the questions that gardening experts face. And interestingly, they do vary regionally. For the moulds, bugs and beasts that cause plant problems respond to cold and warmth just as we do. Many of the diseases caused by bacteria, for instance, are relatively rare in the North; many of the fungal diseases that are dependent upon dampness are infrequent in drier, eastern areas. This is all part of the expert's challenge.

Being a plant pathologist has much in common with being a doctor or perhaps a vet. You must use your experience to gauge the underlying causes of the visible symptoms. And although you can't question the patient, you can certainly talk to its owner. But whereas a doctor has the problems of only one species to consider, the plant pathologist might be faced with any of around 70,000 cultivated plant species and varieties. This is where experience is vital. No-one has seen more than a few of the total number of plants, let alone all their ailments and afflictions. But I find it rather unusual if I haven't seen something similar. And as the years go by, so this fund of knowledge grows, although I can still be surprised. This has been the fascination of *Gardening Britain*; its ability to uncover the unexpected and the novel and so add to the pool of experience. And I do think that gardening experts, like fine wines, improve with age; although unlike some wines, they are also the better for travelling.

AT THE COAST

Gardening in Cornwall and the West is dominated by three features: gardening by the sea, gardening with relatively mild winters and gardening on acidic soils. Together, they give rise to a garden style and range of plants that, while distinct, can all be adapted to suit other regions of the country.

How acidic soils develop

UNDERSTANDING SOIL conditions is one of the keys to successful gardening. My first aim is to explain how acidic soils develop, their distribution in Britain and their gardening characteristics.

Acidity is a term that gardeners use freely, generally in relation to soil. And I'm sure that anyone who has ever experienced school chemistry lessons will know that it has at least something to do with alkalinity, that it is not only a characteristic of soils (lemon juice and vinegar are two other everyday expressions of it) and that it may or may not be a good thing. But for many gardeners, that is about as far as their knowledge goes.

Acidity and alkalinity are the opposite ends of a chemical spectrum. It's useful to know that the spectrum is most readily represented by a scale called pH and there's no need to plumb its chemical depths to know that the scale runs from 0 (extremely acid) to 14 (extremely alkaline) with the mid-point, 7, being neutral (neither one nor the other). But these extremes are only of interest to chemists (concentrated hydrochloric acid, for example, has a pH of about 1) and soil pH covers a much narrower range. The extremes in Britain are about 3.5 for a Sphagnum peat and about 8 for a thin soil overlying chalk, such as on the South Downs.

All soils contain varying amounts of mineral particles and organic matter. Both can contribute to soil acidity. The mineral particles in soil are derived from rocks that have been worn down over many thousands of years by wind, water, frost and other elements. If the original rock was acidic, then by and large the resulting soil will be acidic. Geologically, Britain is exceedingly complex and varied, but

Can I reduce the acidity of my soil so that I can grow some plants that are less successful in acid conditions?

An acidic soil, and especially an acidic soil in a mild area, is a wondrous thing in the range of plants, and especially of trees and shrubs, that it enables you to grow. But it doesn't enable you to grow everything. Some rather important garden ornamentals (roses and clematis to name two) simply won't thrive, while most vegetables and fruit really need a soil that is only just on the acidic side. Fortunately, it's a good deal easier to reduce soil acidity than

it's a fair and rough generalisation to say that most of the older rocks lie to the west (the west of England and the west of Scotland especially) and the younger ones to the east. And it's also generally true that most of the older rocks, which began life in prehistoric volcanoes or deep within the earth's crust, are acidic. Granite is the most familiar example. This is why there are large areas of acidic soils in the far west of both England (Cornwall in particular) and Scotland.

Nonetheless, acidic soils can sometimes occur even if the underlying rock is alkaline. There are areas of acidic soil, for instance, within the great limestone band that extends across central England. This occurs if the vegetation on these sites in the past has lived and died in wet, boggy conditions that permit only partial decomposition (see box, pages 32-33). Peat then forms and in areas of high rainfall, all alkaline minerals are washed away or, to use the correct term, leached.

There are two reasons why acidity in soil is so important and these explain how it influences the types of plants that grow there. First is the plants' relative tolerance of high or low levels of calcium because, at least in Britain, an acid soil contains little calcium, whereas an alkaline soil contains a great deal: chalk and limestone, for example, are relatively pure forms of calcium carbonate. Plants that are highly intolerant of calcium are called calcifuges; those that are highly tolerant are called calcicoles. And although many plants have no strong reaction either way (which is why many of the garden weeds are the same in different areas, irrespective of soil type), it is very often the occurrence of plants with strongly calcicole or calcifuge characteristics that gives both natural and cultivated vegetation its typical appearance. Hence rhododendrons and heathers on acid soils.

to raise it and provided your soil isn't extremely acidic (by which I mean a pH of less than about 4), and provided you don't want to treat your entire garden, a satisfactory solution lies with lime.

By adding lime to an acidic soil, you will go some way towards neutralising it but you should add the lime in amounts that also take account of soil acidity. You should aim to increase the pH to 6.5 (that is, to reduce the acidity) which is the optimum for good plant growth.

You may see different types of limes for sale (quicklime and slaked lime for instance) but finely ground limestone (sometimes called simply garden lime) is to be preferred; it's gentler and more controllable in its action. But always carry out a pH test with a simple kit before adding the lime, apply it in the autumn and never apply it at the same time as fresh animal manures as there will inevitably be a release and build up of ammonia. Allow at least one month to pass between the two operations.

The second reason why soil acidity affects plants is related to the nutrient content. Although it's rather rare in Britain for soils to have a real deficiency in any mineral nutrients, the element manganese can be in short supply in acidic soils and have particularly noticeable effects on vegetables and fruits, such as potatoes and raspberries. More generally important is that all nutrients are more readily absorbed by plants in slightly acidic conditions than in alkaline or strongly acidic ones. On balance, an acidic soil is much more a blessing than a curse in its effect on a gardener's activities; if for no other reason than that it is far, far easier to reduce extreme acidity than extreme alkalinity.

The rhododendron

NO ONE PLANT more exemplifies the garden on acidic soil than the evergreen 'rose tree', *Rhododendron*. There are some 800 species in a huge, magnificent and astonishingly diverse genus that now also embraces both

BELOW: *The variety within the genus* Rhododendron *is astonishing; but the hybrids derived from the Himalayan* Rhododendron arboreum *tend to be among the strongest growing and most hardy.*

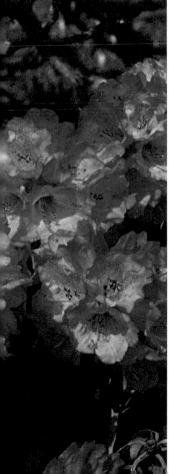

RIGHT: *Few ground cover plants for acidic (and indeed other) soils offer more appeal than cyclamen, with their beautiful small flowers in pinks and white and their bold green leaves, often attractively marbled. See box, page 20.*

evergreen and deciduous azaleas. British gardeners have taken to rhododendrons enthusiastically, yet they belong to a quite alien genus, with no species native to the British Isles. Even the familiar 'wild', purple-flowered *Rhododendron ponticum*, the black sheep of the group in its role as a woody, albeit very beautiful weed, isn't native. Its home is in the eastern Mediterranean and it came to us as recently as the mid-eighteenth century.

But although *Rhododendron* species do occur in many temperate and sub-tropical parts of the world, the northern hemisphere especially, it is south-east Asia that is their spiritual home. And it was for this reason that rhododendrons were the goals of many of the plant collectors who visited China, Nepal, Burma and India. Sir William Hooker and his son Sir Joseph, in turn Directors of the Royal Botanic Gardens at Kew, were rhododendron enthusiasts. It was Hooker *filius* who produced one of the most enduringly beautiful of all illustrated botanical books, *Rhododendrons of Sikkim-Himalaya*, in which he described many of the superb species that he found on his early collecting expeditions in the years immediately before 1850.

The heads of the generally large, trumpet-shaped rhododendron flowers are familiar in their many garden forms, but they do display a number of variations and those with bell-shaped blooms, like 'Bow Bells' or 'Corona', always attract particular attention. Nor should it be forgotten that the evergreen foliage can be at least as great a virtue. Many species display an appealing brown woolly covering of hairs, or indumentum, beneath the leaves, which can themselves range in size from the tiny, almost box-like foliage of the dwarf *Rhododendron impeditum*, a fine plant for the rock garden, to the giant 60cm long fronds of that exquisite plant, *Rhododendron sino-grande*.

And although we tend to think of rhododendrons as medium-sized shrubs, some are dwarf and many, like *Rhododendron sino-grande*, tree-sized. It's to the far west of Britain that you must go, however, to see them in their true proportions. In the wild, rhododendrons tend to be plants of moist mountainous areas where, depending on their size, large numbers occur among alpine meadows or make up the flora of high-altitude forests. The greatest range of species can be grown under cultivation in regions with moist, fairly cool climates, little likelihood of damaging spring frosts and, of course, acid soils. In Britain, it is only species that come from New Guinea and its nearby regions that, intolerant of winter cold, elude us for outdoor growing.

Rhododendrons have been particularly amenable to cultivation, as evident in their propensity to hybridise or cross-breed. As a result over 1000

What is the cause of little notches on the edges of the leaves of my rhododendrons and other evergreens?

Whenever you see small notches around leaf edges, some pest activity is almost certainly the cause. The symptom gives you a clue to the precise creature responsible. Neat, semi-circular notches are the work of the leaf-cutter bee, rather ragged ones generally indicate caterpillars or possibly, if there are slime trails present, slugs or snails. But a pattern of deep, slightly sinuous notches is diagnostic for the vine weevil.

All gardeners must have heard of the vine weevil for it has become one of the great garden pests of our time. Normally, it is the little, off-white, C-shaped, soil-inhabiting larvae that cause the damage by attacking the roots of cyclamen, fuchsia, primula and other plants.

The leaf damage, however, is caused not by the larvae but by the adults; dark grey, characteristically long-snouted beetles. They tend to be nocturnal and so are rather rarely seen and, unusually for beetles of any sort, they are unable to fly. During the daytime they scuttle back into the leaf litter and other debris beneath the shrubs. And it's there that they are best tackled, by thoroughly raking an insecticide dust in and through the litter. Biological controls are not effective against the adults.

An alternative, if you have relatively few shrubs in your garden, is to lay sheets of newspaper beneath the affected plants during the daytime and then go out at night and shine a bright light onto them. The weevils will drop from the leaves onto the newspaper and can then all be collected up in the paper and destroyed.

hybrids are currently available and considerably more have existed in the past. In many respects, hybridising and selection have produced plants of greater hardiness and most of the rhododendrons now obtainable at garden centres belong to the 'hardy hybrid' group. Propagation is easy for the professional nurserymen with the perfect facilities for grafting and for striking cuttings in moist conditions; it is rather more frustrating for the amateur gardener. In gardens layering, or pegging down, of low growing branches is a more reliable method. It does require a great deal of patience, however, for it can be 12 or even 18 months, before rooting takes place and the branch is severed from its parent.

They are undemanding plants, in need of no routine pruning (although the careful removal of dead flower heads is usually beneficial), little feeding (an early season dressing with a balanced rose fertiliser will help) and are generally blessed with long life. Perhaps the commonest explanation for why they do not perform as well as might be expected is the very simple and avoidable fact that they have, initially, been planted too deeply.

Their only disadvantages are a number of pest and disease problems. Vine weevils (see box) and a leaf hopper insect that carries with it the spores of a bud-infecting fungus are the most significant pests, while the recent spread, in Britain, of rhododendron mildew means that it is now potentially more serious than leaf spotting, which occurs on rhododendrons in cultivation. But none of these is serious enough to detract from their immense value and great beauty and they are plants that will clearly continue to bless places with acidic soils as long as men and women continue to garden them.

Great Cornish gardens

'GO WEST, YOUNG MAN' wasn't only a nineteenth-century maxim for the gold prospectors of North America. At more or less the same time as California attracted men and women with its promise of mineral wealth, the west of Britain, and especially the wild and beautiful county of Cornwall was attracting plantsmen and gardeners. They, too, were lured by the promise of riches, but not the riches of shiny yellow metal. It was the horticultural riches offered by a tapering peninsula bathed by the Gulf Stream to produce a mild, if occasionally wild, climate, and by its soils, both fertile and old. For Cornwall exemplifies perfectly the effect of ancient acidic rocks in shaping the soil and landscape.

With its gardeners capitalising on the vast quantities of new and splendid species being brought back from many parts of the world by contemporary plant collectors, Cornwall became a gardening Nirvana. Its gardens are numberless; even the great gardens created there over the decades are to be counted in their dozens. And even those that have survived to delight us today must surely outnumber those of any other area of comparable size in the British Isles. I can only touch on some personal favourites but I hope that in their contrasting features these three offer something of the horticultural flavour of Cornwall.

LEFT: *The view down the deep valley of Trebah to the sea has few equals, even among the many other magnificent gardens of Cornwall.*

Trebah is one of the creations of a Cornish gardening dynasty, a Falmouth shipping family called Fox. They created six great gardens and it was Charles Fox who first came in 1826 to the deep and romantic 600m long ravine of Trebah that drops away some 60m down to the Helford estuary. Like its twin garden of Glendurgan next door (the creation of Charles' cousin Alfred), it is the individuality of the site that almost wholly determined its construction and content. As with many another Cornish garden, the use of windbreaks was critical. The resilience and worth in this role of the Mediterranean maritime pine, *Pinus pinaster*, has proved itself over the years. Those trees planted in the 1820s are now enormous. Under their protection, Fox was able to grow pretty well all of the plants for which Cornwall has become recognised. There are rhododendrons of course, including the garden's own variety 'Trebah Gem', magnolias, many tender South Americans such as the Chilean laurel, *Laurelia sempervirens*, tree ferns, Chusan palms and that wonderful, lesser-known, yellow-flowered relative of *Cornus kousa*, *Cornus capitata*, also to be seen at the recently resurrected garden of Heligan.

Yet Trebah would no longer exist in its present splendour had not the current owner, Major Tony Hibbert, devoted his time and energies to it since he bought the property in 1981. He came to Cornwall thinking to retire but then realised that his newly acquired, overgrown valley was a neglected gardening gem.

Today, the special appeal to me of Trebah is the sheer richness of the plantings. Unlike some Cornish gardens, the interest doesn't stop with the trees and shrubs. The underplantings of herbaceous perennials and bulbs are equally fine, while the stream that rushes down the

I'm unsuccessful with bulbs in my acidic soil; what do you suggest?

I'm sure the main reason you have failed is simply because you haven't chosen the right types of bulbs. I know that there's a temptation to opt for the more familiar types but whilst these are reliable in most soils, some are less successful in acidic conditions. And yet, especially if your soil is fairly organic, and if you have slightly shaded, woodland conditions, an acid soil enables you to grow a wonderful range of truly splendid bulbous plants. Of the commoner bulbs try those varieties of daffodil and narcissi said to be suitable for naturalising, the larger crocuses, cyclamen and snowdrops. Tulips are generally less satisfactory but among other bulbous plants, I've listed my top five with my recommended varieties:

gorge has provided the wherewithal for a lush and sumptuous water garden. Trebah belies the criticism so often heard, that gardening in Cornwall is gardening with woody plants and gardening for the spring.

Trewithen, approximately the same size as Trebah, also has fine rhododendrons and it too has an important shelter belt. But it differs in being set within a much larger parkland and is topographically quite distinct, as the site is almost flat – a high-level plateau. The park is eighteenth century and its trees provide the shelter for the garden which dates from the early years of the nineteenth century, when George Johnstone inherited the property. Johnstone followed the example of many another Cornish gardener in growing trees and shrubs from seeds brought back by plant collectors, although as he was a little later than some in starting, using seed collected by Forrest, Kingdon Ward and Wilson, rather than Fortune and Hooker.

The greatest glory of Trewithen lies in its magnolias, with which Johnstone was besotted and on which he became a world authority. In truth, although they thrive wonderfully in the richly acidic soil here, it's too commonly believed that they are on a par with rhododendrons and camellias in their need for acidic conditions. They aren't; most will grow perfectly well in soils that are neutral or even slightly alkaline. It is climate that tends to be the more limiting factor. But it can't be denied that, like acers, among others, magnolias certainly grow well and attain a richness in acidic conditions that does give them that little something extra. If, however, you want a souvenir of this garden, then almost no matter what your soil is, and provided you can give it some shelter, you should succeed with something that is much less grand but still a fine plant, such as

Cardiocrinum giganteum (Giant lily). Related to lilies and magnificent in a woodland position, but does need room. 300cm/10ft.

Eranthis hyemalis (Winter aconite). May be difficult to establish from tubers so if possible buy plants that are in leaf. 15cm/6in.

Erythronium species (Dog's tooth violet). Seed is obtainable but rarely comes true so it's better to buy plants. I'd recommend *E. californicum* 'White Beauty'; *E. dens-canis*; *E.* 'Pagoda'; *E. revolutum*. 30cm/12in.

Hyacinthoides non-scripta (Bluebell). Can be invasive so only plant where there is room for it to spread. 50cm/20in.

Trillium species (Wood lily). Rhizomes are expensive and as most types will come true from seed, this is well worth trying. Allow about six months for germination. I'd recommend *T. erectum*; *T. grandiflorum*; *T. grandiflorum flore-pleno*; *T. rivale*. 30cm/12in.

Is there a range of perennials suitable for my mild, coastal garden where salt spray and wind are problems?

Wind and salt spray, of course, are the constant features associated with coastal gardening, although the problems tend to be balanced by the fact that coastal conditions are fairly mild. The selection of plants with tolerance of wind are readily dealt with for you must choose species and varieties that have relatively short, relatively stiff stems and then give them support; even though the same varieties may grow unsupported in more sheltered gardens. Much of the trend in the recent breeding of perennials has been towards stiffer-stemmed varieties which tend to be easier to maintain wherever they are grown and you will find them highlighted in catalogues. For support, you will find the best is that provided by the circular, metal, grid-patterned supports that are positioned on three or four legs over the plants, so that the stems grow through the holes in the grid.

But as with all supports, it's essential that they be in place before the stems elongate.

Tolerance of salt spray is more difficult to select because there are no obvious distinguishing features. It might be thought, for instance, that plants with soft fleshy foliage would be more prone to damage but in truth, many soft-leaved succulents are successful while many tough-leaved and woody types aren't.

Achillea	Geranium
Anemone (Japanese)	Gypsophila
Anthemis	Heuchera
Artemisia	Kniphofia
Aster (Michaelmas daisy)	Mimulus
Bergenia	Oenothera
Campanula	Penstemon
Centaurea	Phygelius
Crambe	Salvia
Dianthus	Santolina
Echinops	Scabiosa
Erigeron	Sedum
Eryngium	Sisyrinchium
Euphorbia	Stachys
Filipendula	Veronica

BULBS

Agapanthus	Iris (rhizomatous, bearded)
Allium	Nerine
Alstroemeria	Schizostylis
Crocosmia	Zantedeschia

RIGHT: *For successful seaside gardening select varieties with natural tolerance of wind and salt spray; and provide them with shelter behind which they can establish and grow.*

Ceanothus arboreus 'Trewithen Blue'. It was raised here and has become recognised in recent years as one of the best of all evergreen varieties of that lovely American shrub, known for its powdery blue flowers in spring.

My third Cornish garden is different again; and not just because it's in the minority in lacking that Cornish prefix 'tre', which means a hamlet. Mount Edgcumbe is vast and lies just inside the eastern boundary of Cornwall overlooking Plymouth Sound. Also a formal parkland garden, it is one of the most beautiful and magnificent in England. But it does still have those important Cornish characteristics of an acid soil and a sheltered maritime climate. It is much older than my first two gardens and probably older as a garden site than any other in Cornwall.

It came into the Edgcumbe family in 1479 and the licence to enclose a deer park here was granted by Henry VIII when the family left their other house of Cotehele (and another magnificent garden), some 6 kilometres up the Tamar valley. Cotehele became a 'small' retreat, Mount Edgcumbe their home, and during the early eighteenth century a formal garden was created, to be swept away some years later as part of the national craving for the 'natural' parkland environment. But formality returned in French, Italian and English styles and it is gardens in these styles that you see today at Mount Edgcumbe. There is much to admire here and much to surprise. Many people don't expect orangeries, parterres, formal yew hedges or statuary in Cornish gardens. Cornwall is thought of as a wild and untamed place where such niceties as clipped shrubs, straight-edged borders and anything geometric do not belong. But they are here at Mount Edgcumbe and they are present, on a less ambitious scale, in other gardens too. They go to prove that given the natural blessings of soil and climate which Cornwall offers, gardeners can do almost anything they fancy.

Annuals generally don't do well in my acidic soil; are there any that you can recommend?

Most of the summer-flowering hardy and half-hardy annuals are fairly tolerant of a wide range of soil types. My experience is that when they don't make a good display in acidic soils, this is more to do with the soil being somewhat

The gardener's rich seashore plant inheritance

I'M NOT SURE what proportion of British gardens are, literally, seaside gardens. But a considerable number fall under the influence of the sea in some respects. Perhaps they are exposed to salt-laden winds in winter; perhaps they are further away but benefit from the warming and weather-smoothing effect of the sea during the winter. There's no doubt however that the coast is both a highly individual and rather unusual environment for plant life, with a number of special features.

Wind, cold or warm, is an important force, but it isn't unique to the coast. Winds, often very strong ones, occur in other places; most notably in mountains. The feature of the seashore that is indisputably special is the presence of salt, in the air and perhaps in the soil. And yet, if you pour salt onto a good many of the plants in your garden, they will soon wither and die. Clearly, coastal plants have learned to tolerate salt. What is so intriguing and serves to demonstrate the adaptability of the plant kingdom, is that we owe the coast a great debt, for a remarkable number of our garden plants originated there. Our gardens, whether or not they contain any salt, would be extremely impoverished without the plant contribution of the shoreline.

Look along the light alkaline sea cliffs of our south and west coasts and you will see a medium-sized, bluish-green leaved, loosely formed but rather familiar plant. It is *Brassica oleracea*, the wild cabbage, progenitor of a whole tribe that includes Brussels sprouts, cauliflowers, broccoli, kohl rabi, kale and others. Its fondness for relatively alkaline soils is one of its garden characteristics: cabbages will never be very successful on acidic sites. But there is no

impoverished than the acidity itself. I think it's worth persevering with all of the familiar types but I suggest that you do four things. First, that you raise or buy plants and put these into the beds rather than sowing directly. Second, raise the plants in a soil-less compost rather than a soil-based type. This is because a soil-based compost will usually be richer than the surrounding soil and the roots may be reluctant to grow outwards. Third, do be sure to feed the plants well. Prepare the planting position thoroughly, if possible by incorporating well rotted compost some time in advance of planting and then raking in a general fertiliser. And finally, feed the plants regularly throughout the growing season with one of the proprietary liquid or soluble fertilisers.

ABOVE: *The natural home of the wild cabbage is on the thin soil of chalk cliffs. But few people recognise this loose-leaved plant as the ancestor of so many kitchen garden vegetables.*

LEFT: *A seaside cottage garden, like all cottage gardens, should display a cheerful, carefree appearance; although this conceals a great deal of hard work and careful selection of plants.*

special need for salt; until they reach the dining table. In the same family, but unique in having retained in its name an affinity for the sea, is seakale, *Crambe maritima*. This is one of those winter vegetables that tended to pass from favour with the coming of the deep freeze and the year-round availability of summer crops that it facilitated. But seakale shoots, blanched to produce a more tender and palatable texture, still make unusual and different eating.

The wild asparagus, *Asparagus officinalis*, is similar enough to garden asparagus to be recognisable, although it almost always occurs on the coast in a prostrate, creeping form called *prostratus*. The garden version, the variety *officinalis*, has now itself become naturalised on the sea coast in a number of areas. And in any event, the resemblance between wild and domestic plants has been noticed for long enough for gardeners to have believed in the past that a liberal dosing of salt was essential to grow good garden asparagus. It isn't, although interestingly, the shortage of potassium fertilisers during the Second World War prompted the widespread use as alternatives of those chemically similar compounds based on sodium, including of course, sodium chloride or common salt.

My soil is basically poor: peaty, stony and very free-draining. How can I improve it?

It doesn't really matter what are the underlying causes, a poor soil is generally poor because it lacks two things: structure and nutrients. The structure of a soil is an expression of the way that the main components (sand, silt, clay and humus) have bound together to form crumbs with air spaces in between. A well-structured soil has a balance of air and solid matter to permit drainage to take place and yet allow sufficient moisture to remain around the crumbs. A poorly structured soil allows water to drain away

The family Umbelliferae, that includes carrots, celery and fennel, is also an important one in the vegetable garden. Several of its members are plants of the coast, although often not recognised as such because we are more used to identifying them by their roots But on the cliff tops, the wild carrot, *Daucus carota*, is often revealed by its white flower and seeding heads. Closely related but requiring quite different conditions is the wild celery, *Apium graveolens*, which, unlike the carrot, is a plant of the wet and is frequently found growing in and alongside the brackish water of coastal ditches. In the Chenopodiaceae, which embraces spinach and beetroot among other garden vegetables, there

too freely, taking nutrients with it; or, alternatively, as with a heavy clay, has too few air spaces and so becomes waterlogged.

The structure of all poor soils can be improved in one important way: by the addition of organic matter. It doesn't matter what form your organic matter takes; manures and good garden composts are generally the best but mushroom compost, finely pulverised bark and other proprietary materials are close behind. These substances contain natural glues that help to bind together the mineral particles of the soil while providing masses of minute moisture-retaining sponges in the form of the broken-down plant cellular matter they contain.

Low nutrient content of soil is readily put right by the use of balanced fertilisers every season. But always remember that in a free-draining soil, these will be lost more rapidly and will therefore need replenishing more frequently (see pages 58-61).

are also several coastal members. The sea beet itself, *Beta vulgaris*, recognisably similar to the garden plant, is among the most salt-tolerant. It is one of the plants that you will find among the wave-washed spots, especially among shingle, closest to the sea.

But if the coast has contributed importantly to the kitchen garden, it has also given us numerous garden ornamentals. Indeed, almost every flowering plant that you see on the seashore and cliffs has its garden counterpart. From the spring squills, *Scilla*, on the cliff tops to the sea asters, *Aster tripolium*, on the sides of the cliff face, down past the thrifts and campions to the horned poppies, *Glaucium flavum*, on the drift line itself, the flower garden's debt to the seashore is immense.

And the coast has contributed its share of shrubs too. The most typical and familiar must be the pink-flowered tamarisk, *Tamarix gallica*, in reality an alien from the Mediterranean, that has become naturalised along our coasts. It is probably the most exposure-tolerant of all flowering shrubs, remarkably so considering that it is evergreen, and it is used extensively for stabilising sand and shingle. The sea buckthorn, *Hippophae rhamnoides*, is another coastal shrub, increasingly appreciated as a tough garden plant, in inland as well as coastal sites. And provided both male and female plants are grown, you may expect a striking and characteristic crop of orange berries later in the year that contrast so appealingly with the silver, elongated willow-like leaves.

The virtue that has, I think, made these and many other coastal plants so popular is their ability to thrive in light, dry soils. It is this, beyond their salt-tolerance, that makes them so valuable in summer gardens, especially so when garden owners go on holiday and must leave their plants untended for a couple of weeks or more.

Soft and shady ferns

ON THE FACE of it, a plant that never produces flowers and occurs in shades of green would seem to offer little in visual or any other gardening terms. The truth is very different when the plants in question are ferns and in wetter, milder gardens they tend to play the role of ground cover, woodland understorey or wall plants, elsewhere played by evergreen shrubs.

Ferns have always held an inherent fascination for me since early schooldays when I took delight in recreating in pie-dishes, miniatures of the landscapes of geological ages past. Sandy deserts with model dinosaurs sufficed for certain periods and replicas of ancient seashores for others. But for the coal swamps of the Carboniferous period, I simply went into the garden and found sprigs of ferns and of their allies, *Equisetum species* or horsetails, with their strange and simple stems and spiky foliage. For they are plants that in fundamental appearance have changed little in tens of millions of years. Ferns populated the earth long before flowering plants evolved and their lack of flowers and absence of seeds is more than compensated for by a rich variety of frond form and size.

In gardening, ferns have waxed and waned in popularity. They probably reached their zenith during the Victorian period when both

RIGHT: *The origin of most tree ferns lies in New Zealand and Tasmania yet they have adapted so well to the mild, acidic gardens of the west of Britain that these could now easily pass for their natural homes.*

tender species for indoors and hardier ones for outside were collected with a passion that has never been equalled. They declined during the early years of the twentieth century when plant breeders were turning out such great variety in flowering plants. But the pendulum has begun to swing again and today an ever-increasing range of hardy ferns, both deciduous and ever-green (or winter green as fern enthusiasts tend to describe them) is available. And if any garden, anywhere, can have a representative collection, the milder, wetter gardens of the west can have them in amazing variety.

Although the world total of fern species is large (8-12,000, depending on who you ask), the vast majority are tropical and the number of species hardy in Britain is relatively small. There are moreover only about 50 native species but they more than make up for this in the incredible number of varieties. Yes, ferns both as species and as a group are extremely variable and they range in size from one of the smallest of all green plants, the floating fern *Azolla* which covers the surface of ponds and turns such an attractive rich red in autumn, to species that attain the height of small trees.

My garden has a peaty soil that I expected to be highly acidic; why isn't it?

I think you have fallen into the common trap of assuming that all peat and all peat-based soils are the same. They aren't, and there are several different types of peat. All comprise the part-decomposed remains of plant material; it is important that they are only part-decomposed because this means that the plants lived and, more pertinently died, in waterlogged conditions conducive to limited anaerobic but little aerobic decomposition. Of the various peat types, some that are very significant in other parts of the world (the saw sedge peats of the south-eastern United States for instance) are of little significance in Britain where there are two main peat types, broadly called moss peat and sedge peat.

It is the so-called tree ferns that are so striking and form such a characteristic part of the vegetation of Cornish gardens; and indeed, to a degree, of areas of the local woodland too, for some have naturalised and look as much at home there as in their native New Zealand and Tasmania. It was the tree ferns moreover that first took the eye of the gardeners who stumbled on the overgrown remains of the great Cornish garden of Heligan and persuaded them that here was something worthy of saving and resurrection. They are remarkable plants and what passes for the trunk is, in truth, simply a pile of old frond bases, built up over many

In Britain, moss peat invariably means peat derived from species of the bog moss, Sphagnum, although in some parts of the world other types of moss are important too. Sphagnum peat is fibrous and very light, generally brown in colour, with an extremely high water-holding capacity (it really is the most remarkable sponge, holding up to ten times its own weight of water), and a pH of 3.5-4. Sedge peat is derived from sedges (species of *Carex*), heather (*Calluna vulgaris*) and certain bog grasses, especially the common reed (*Phragmites australis*) and harestail cotton grass (*Eriophorum vaginatum*). It is more highly decomposed than Sphagnum peat, with a lower water-holding capacity (about three times its own weight), dark brown or black in colour and a higher pH. The pH range of sedge peat usually lies on the acidic side of neutral but in certain circumstances, as in the East Anglian fens, where the fen water has drained from calcareous rocks like chalk and limestone, it can even be alkaline in reaction. And this is when gardeners become really puzzled.

years and on top of which the plant itself grows, passing its roots downwards through the column of dead material to the soil below.

Few ferns will tolerate dry conditions, or indeed alkaline ones, the native polypody, *Polypodium vulgare*, being the commonest exception in both respects. This is because the fern frond, in its generally highly indented appearance, perfectly epitomises the twin features that all green plants attempt. Leaves or fronds are always a compromise between exposing the maximum amount of green tissue to the sun to enable photosynthesis and food manufacture to take place, and permitting some water loss by evaporation but not allowing too much moisture to be dissipated. The relatively huge surface area is needed to enable ferns to obtain sufficient light in a woodland. But this does mean that they really succeed only in wet places where the atmosphere itself is laden with abundant moisture, so evaporation stays within bounds.

Among my particular favourites are many that do well in Cornish gardens, such as the numerous varieties of *Polystichum setiferum* or *Dryopteris affinis*.

Homes and gardens: how they fit together

GERTRUDE JEKYLL, the gardener, designer and artist of blessed memory, wrote a number of gardening books, some of which are still read. The one that I have referred to more often than any of the others was published almost a century ago, in 1900, and yet its message, still relevant today, is

often overlooked. The book was called *Home and Garden* and it was written in response to many requests to set down her views on the inter-relationship of garden with house. It was a particularly appropriate work for a gardener and plantswoman who had come to realise in the creation of her own home at Munstead Wood in Surrey how gardens and houses are so inextricably related. And it was fitting too for a woman who worked so closely with an architect; in her case, arguably the outstanding British architect of the century, Edwin Lutyens. I certainly don't want to harp on about Gertrude for I don't agree with everything that she wrote, but suffice it to say that another of her books was *Gardens for Small Country Houses*. In truth, 'small' was a relative term and few people today have homes anything like as large as those she described in her book, but the message remains.

On my travels it's my pleasure and delight to visit many gardens, great and small, and I see examples in both categories that blend perfectly with the house and others that have no sympathetic relationship with each other whatever, the one appearing to be

LEFT: *The Great Terrace of Athelhampton with its obelisks of yew, so cleverly reflecting other features in the garden and in the buildings too.*

bolted on to the other. Among gardens that the public can visit, the West of England provides good examples of both. Interestingly, what is arguably my favourite garden in England, Hestercombe in Somerset, is a Jekyll and Lutyens collaboration but the house isn't Lutyens. It's an earlier edifice and there is no better example of disharmony; the pleasure of the garden is only really to be enjoyed when one averts one's gaze from the property that overlooks it.

Sometimes, the house is rather remote from the garden and plays no important role, as at Knightshayes Court in Devon. Here, in what has been described to me as a Scottish tradition, a walled garden with associated herbaceous borders, a magnificent avenue of Douglas firs, fruit orchard and formal hedges, was built during this century, well away from the big Victorian house. The two are equally, but separately splendid; a fine enough concept if you have the room.

In other instances, by contrast, the house and garden are totally at one and the glorious

How can I create a small, low-maintenance garden for my seaside holiday cottage which I only visit a few times a year?

A low-maintenance garden, at the seaside or anywhere else, is a garden that lacks annuals and lacks vegetables, since both require attention. If it is only to be visited on a few occasions each year, it should also lack any of the perennials that require routine staking. The operations that can be done therefore are once- or twice-a-year feeding, an annual pruning, lifting and dividing. Two groups of plants will provide

and ancient property of Athelhampton in Dorset is a gem in this respect. And yet what is so curious at Athelhampton is that some four centuries separate the building of the house from the creation of the garden. They look contemporary, so perfectly harmonious are they, but it was the skill of the gardener, Inigo Thomas, in the nineteenth century that achieved this.

Although not a unique feature, the abiding memory of Athelhampton is its Corona, a circular enclosure from which gateways open out on four sides. In its centre is a circular pool with a fountain. Gardening in the round is never easy but Thomas achieved it here magnificently, for through each of the gateways is a view luring you into other parts of the garden. Nearby for instance is the Great Terrace, with a sunken lawn around which 12 huge

interest and colour with this minimal attention and I suggest that you make your selections from a wide range of shrubs and, provided your garden is reasonably exposed, alpines.

The reason that I stress exposure if you want to grow a selection of alpines in your seaside garden is that many of them are prone to rotting in situations of high humidity. The bulk of your planting will therefore come from shrubs and in a small garden, dwarf bush and ground cover types should take priority. The following list will offer you some suggestions:

Atriplex canescens
A. halimus
Brachyglottis (Senecio) 'Sunshine'
Bupleurum fruticosum
Cassinia fulvida
Choisya ternata
Corokia cotoneaster
Cotoneaster (all smaller forms)
Cytisus (all smaller forms)

Ephedra andina
E. distachya
Euonymus fortunei
Fabiana imbricata 'Prostrata'
Fuchsia magellanica 'Pumila'
Genista (all smaller forms)
Halimium (all)
Hebe (all smaller forms)
Helianthemum (all)
Helichrysum (all)
Hydrangea macrophylla (smaller varieties)
Ilex aquifolium
Lavandula spica
Lonicera pileata
Olearia (Pachystegia) insignis
Olearia (smaller species)
Ozothamnus ledifolius
Parahebe (all)
Pyracantha (all)
Rosmarinus officinalis
Santolina (all)
Spiraea (smaller varieties)

obelisks of yew reflect the shape of the stone obelisks surrounding the Corona itself, which in turn reflect the pointed roofs of two summerhouses.

I hope that here, as I find myself saying so often, the home gardener can learn from the great and that effects such as these will stimulate all gardeners to be enterprising. Let's not only plant for this month or next but have the foresight to make at least some features that will mature over the years. We aren't all fortunate enough to live in Athelhampton but I feel that when we create our own gardens, we should do so by looking long and hard first at the house. Let's not put stark aluminium greenhouses in front of Victorian bay windows or impose ridiculous formality around a thatched village cottage.

WATERWISE GARDENING

*East Anglia is flat and East Anglia
is dry. Neither of these familiar notions is
entirely true and there is some relatively
high ground, in Suffolk especially,
although overall this is certainly
an area of little rainfall. And it is largely
because of this that its gardeners are
especially challenged to be at their
most inventive. There is much we can
learn from them.*

Too wet or too dry: why?

I THINK IT'S UNLIKELY that, in any part of the British Isles, you would be unable to grow a particular type of plant just because the rainfall was too high. And, conversely, there's probably no area where the annual rainfall is inadequate for any type of plant, given that other climatic factors are suitable. Nonetheless, as every gardener knows, rain never seems to be falling when it is needed and always seems to be falling when it is least wanted. And the most marked discrepancies between the amounts of rainfall in the different seasons tend to occur between those high, western districts with the highest total rainfall, and the drier parts in the east of England which, in general, have a more uniform monthly distribution (see map, page 7)

PREVIOUS PAGE: Hostas, geraniums, heucheras, lamiums, alchemilla and ligularias here offer as rich planting as you could wish for.

The rain that falls during the growing season is of greatest importance to gardeners and it is within this spring-summer period that small monthly, weekly or daily fluctuations can be most significant. And overall figures can be misleading. Superficially, a July rainfall of 58mm, such as that shown for Cambridge, may seem quite adequate for gardens, but it may all have fallen during two thunderstorms on, say, the 8th and 22nd of the month. Technically therefore, there has been no drought, (see page 44 for the definition of a drought) but with high temperatures and high evaporation rates, this amount of rain will have had little effect on plant growth.

Bear in mind that one square metre of leaf cover may lose over 5 litres of water per day in the summer, and this amount will need to be replaced in the soil. Yet that 58mm of rainfall represents only about 32 litres of rain per square metre for the whole month.

The variations across the country in avail-

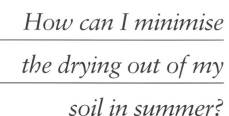

How can I minimise the drying out of my soil in summer?

Soils dry out for three reasons: first, because water drains away into the subsoil and beyond; second, because there is evaporation at its surface; and third, because there is evaporation from the leaf surface of plants. One material, one very valuable garden material, can minimise the first two. Compost, manure or other organic matter offers all of the benefits of improved soil structure (see box, pages 28-29) and in addition its sponge-like properties help prevent too much water from draining away.

ability of water for gardening in recent years have highlighted these regional differences. Some variation is undoubtedly due to varying efficiency on the part of the regional water companies. But underlying this, there are natural factors beyond the control of anyone. If there is moisture-laden air present, then particular combinations of circumstances, or of topographical and geographical features, will cause rain to fall. If it isn't, they won't. A glance at the map on page 7 will show just how great the regional differences in annual rainfall are and, in general, you will see that the nearer that any one place is to the ocean and/or to high ground, the more rain there will be.

What usually happens is that warm, westerly or south-westerly winds pass over the Atlantic Ocean and cause water to evaporate. This produces the moisture-laden air that I mentioned. When this air reaches the high land of the west and central parts of the country, it rises, cools and expands. The moisture condenses, clouds form, and rain falls.

This is called relief rain or orobatic rain. But that doesn't fully explain this variation in rainfall. There are two other important types of rainfall which are much less constant and predictable in their occurrence and because of this, they often cause more problems to gardeners.

Cyclonic rain is produced in the low pressure systems that you will see nightly on the television weather forecast maps. Here, warm and moist air from the south blows northwards and rises above cold and dense polar air moving southwards. As with relief rainfall, the rising moist air expands and cools, but with the significant difference that cyclonic rain can occur over low as well as high ground. Moreover, unlike mountains, low pressure systems are constantly moving, and so outbreaks of cyclonic rain are much harder to predict; as any weather forecaster will be happy to use as an explanation for a mistake.

Finally, there is the least predictable of all; convectional or thunder rain. Here, localised

But laid as a blanket up to 10cm thick over the soil in the early part of the season, whilst the ground is still moist, it will cut down evaporation loss at the soil surface too.

If organic matter is unavailable, then lay synthetic, plastic mulching sheet instead. It's less attractive although just as effective but again, must be laid when there is already moisture in the soil. Mulching a dry soil will simply keep it dry.

Loss of moisture through the leaves of plants can be minimised by growing no more plants than you really need; remember that a square metre of leaf surface can lose up to 5 litres of water per day in the height of summer. Here, too, mulching is useful to suppress weeds. And, by the same token, keeping down weed growth will also minimise water loss through leaves.

Lily bulbs are very expensive to buy: is there an inexpensive way of multiplying lilies?

It's important first to choose the best quality bulbs. Because of limitations imposed by transportation and marketing, they are often not available to buy until several weeks after they have been lifted. Do be sure therefore that they aren't at all shrivelled or pinched.

There are several ways in which the stock can be increased. By seed is the simplest although different lilies vary in the ease with which their seed will germinate, and many hybrids of course will not come true. I have had the best success with *Lilium regale*, fortunately my favourite lily. I sow the seed as fresh as possible. If you can obtain a ripe seed pod from a friend you are more likely to have success than with packeted seed. It is best to sow the seed as soon as it is visible – when the pod begins to split open in late summer. I sow thinly in a soil-based seedling compost; lilies resent the disturbance caused by thinning out. I have had seed-raised plants of *Lilium regale* in flower within two years.

Each lily bulb comprises a group of overlapping fleshy scales which can be pulled away and used to produce new plants. Press each scale, tip upwards, into a box of seedling compost and keep this in a warm place until green shoots appear. Then pot up the young plant and expect flowers within three years. But don't take more than four or five scales from each bulb.

Clumps of established bulbs can be lifted and divided every few years; replant them as deeply as before. Some types of lily, especially tiger lilies, produce small black bulbs or bulbils at the stem base or in the joint between the leaf and the stem. These should be removed after the flowers have faded but before they drop to the ground. Sow them with their tips just below the surface in a soil-based seedling compost and the plants should flower within three or four years.

heating of the earth gives rise to powerful upcurrents of warm, moist air. The result is towering clouds, up to 6,000m high, in which large raindrops form, buoyed up by the rising air. Lightning and thunder often accompany convectional rain, hence its common name of thunder rain. This very heavy, if short-lived, rainfall can have considerable localised impact in gardens through its sheer physical force: flowers and vegetation are beaten down or broken, and the soil may become compacted. There may also be the more insidious splashing upwards of soil onto low-hanging fruits, causing them to rot. But in terms of annual rainfall and the alleviation of drought, thunder rain is of relatively little importance.

In Britain, as I'm sure we all discovered during 1995, a drought is officially a period of at least 15 days when no measurable rain has fallen. A part of the country that annually has a consistently low rainfall isn't necessarily likely to suffer the most droughts, and there are some regional variations. The occurrence of periods of drought is notoriously hard to predict in the long term, but as I've indicated, the absence of moisture-laden air means no rain, wherever you live. And in 1995, the winds were blowing consistently, not from the wet ocean to the west, but from the dry land masses of the east and south.

But finally, what about snow? The proportion of the annual precipitation that falls as snow also varies across the country, but in the lowlands, even in areas such as Scotland where snow falls on average on 35 days each year, the proportion of moisture that it contributes to gardens isn't very much. When, last winter, heavy snowfalls followed the 1995 summer drought, the water companies were very quick to remind us that 25cm of snow represents only 2.5cm of rain. It takes a good deal of snow to fill a reservoir.

Bulbs, corms and tubers

PLANTS ARE CLEVER things. They might not talk or run around but they have certainly acquired a great deal of know-how about survival. And like people with deep freezes and squirrels with nuts, they have discovered the need to lay in food supplies as and when they are available, to be drawn on in times of scarcity. During the winter, life gets tough above ground and many plants retreat below soil level. And it's on the wide flat lands of East Anglia that the impact of this retreat is seen as

My daffodils regularly come up 'blind', with no flowers. What causes this?

The commonest reason is that initially the bulbs were planted too shallowly. Gardeners seem afraid that with deep planting the shoots won't be able to reach the soil surface. In reality, the roots establish better, the plant is better able to take up water and nutrients and so form good flower buds and becomes, overall, a much more robust individual. As a rule of thumb, you should plant bulbs with their base at a depth equal to between two and a half and three times their diameter, but it's better to err on the deeper, rather than the shallower side.

But although incorrect planting is the commonest cause of flower failure, there are others. Choosing a variety such as some of

dramatically as anywhere. For among the most important plants of the region are daffodils, potatoes and carrots. In spring or summer, you can't miss them. In winter, there's nothing to be seen; and the reason and explanation lies with a group of plant structures called bulbs, corms, tubers and rhizomes. They are among the most important plant groups in gardening yet we take them for granted, don't give them the care that they merit and very often don't make the most of the potential they offer.

For many gardeners, the terms bulb, corm, tuber and rhizome are more or less interchangeable. They tend to be grouped together in most gardening books and they certainly are in most of the ornamental plant catalogues. Botanically, however, they are interestingly different.

A bulb is a specialised type of shoot in which the leaves are closely folded over each other and swell in order to store food reserves for the young plant. The stem on which the leaves are borne is reduced in size and shape to a flattened, plate-like structure at the base, and from this modified stem the roots arise. So even though no roots may be present when bulbs are planted, it's important to place this flat plate downwards in the soil. Some bulbs (onions, narcissi and tulips, for example) have swollen leaves closely covering the entire structure, with the outermost leaves reduced to papery scales. In other bulb types (lilies are the best-known examples), the swollen scales are more loosely overlapping and have no papery outer layer. Small buds form at the base of a parent bulb, and from these, daughter bulbs develop. In narcissi, for example, the old and new bulbs remain attached, and eventually a large mass develops which should be split up every few years as it becomes a congested

the doubles or split-corolla types that isn't suitable for naturalising will lead to disappointment, while failure to feed the plants after the previous season's flowering can weaken them. As soon as the blooms fade, the plants should be given liquid fertiliser two or three times during the succeeding six week period. Feeding can then stop and the foliage be cut down.

Virus infection can also bring about flower failure although there will be some other abnormal feature of the plants such as yellow streaks on the leaves. Other diseases may be responsible, root decay especially, but this is only likely on heavy wet soils and the overall growth will be poor and the root rotting very obvious when a few bulbs are dug up for inspection. Pests of various types can be to blame. Eelworms and other soil-inhabiting creatures will damage bulbs, although they are readily evident. Attacks by the narcissus fly are common. This fly gains entry to the bulb down the hole that remains after the flower stalk and leaves have shrivelled. It can be prevented from doing this by raking soil over the holes.

mass. In other plants, the old, parent bulb dies, leaving one or two slightly smaller offspring.

A corm is structurally more simple than a bulb, and is a solid, swollen stem that also serves the purpose of storing food. Superficially, some corms look much like bulbs, but they have a bud at the top, not within. One or more (or as in gladioli, many more) daughter corms are formed below the parent during growth. These should be carefully separated when the corms are lifted at the end of the season. They are best replanted in pots initially, carefully nurtured for two or three years until they attain flowering size and then planted out again.

Some plants, such as potatoes, dahlias and peonies, produce swollen storage organs that are neither bulbs nor corms, but tubers. There are two different types of tuber and they can be distinguished by looking at the position of their buds. Potato tubers are stem tubers and have buds or 'eyes' over a large part of the surface, and it is these that sprout before planting in the spring. The fact that potato tubers can turn green also indicates that they are stems. Roots don't turn green and so the tubers of dahlias and peonies are root tubers: swollen fibrous roots with buds only at the top. The carrot is a swollen tap root as opposed to swollen lateral or fibrous roots.

And finally, there are rhizomes. Many plants produce them; they are stems that creep along the surface, often rooting at intervals. In a few types of plant these too can be swollen as food storage organs and the lovely summer-flower-ing bearded border irises, such as those at The Abbey in Eye, Suffolk, are the best examples.

So we have a wide variety of plant structures, all serving more or less the same purpose. All have in common a mass of rather soft fleshy tissue. This means that they are prone to rotting and, with few exceptions, they won't thrive in wet or waterlogged conditions. So when ornamental bulbs and

ABOVE: *The underground storage tuber of the peony (*Paeonia mollis*) belies the beauty of the flowers that will arise each year in spring.*

corms are planted, it always makes sense to lay a handful of sand underneath and so improve drainage. But do remember that uniformity of appearance can be deceptive, for all of these storage organs share the relative hardiness and tenderness characteristics of other plant parts. Some will survive frosts, some won't and must be lifted for storage. Potato tubers are among those that survive, so it always amazes me how, year after year, vegetable gardeners take such care and trouble to lift and store their potatoes away from the frost. And year after year, the ability of the soil itself to protect them becomes apparent when stray tubers overlooked in the ground from last year's crop sprout forth to produce annoying new plants among this season's vegetables.

Great East Anglian gardens

IT COMES AS a surprise for many people to discover that Victorian horticulturists didn't invent the herbaceous border. Certainly, they made excellent use of it and brought it to the attention of far more gardeners, but its history goes back a great deal further. The oldest herbaceous borders that I know of are those at Arley Hall in Cheshire. Like all good herbaceous borders of course, their plants, whilst perennial, aren't immortal and replanting must take place every few years. Today, the herbaceous border has largely been replaced in home gardens by mixed borders, comprising both herbaceous plants and shrubs. These are less labour intensive (think of all of that tying up and staking needed in borders devoted solely to herbaceous plants) and they also offer some interest in the winter, provided by the shrubs, particularly the evergreens.

But there's no denying that the herbaceous border, well-planted and maintained, is one of the great glories of the English garden and Helmingham Hall, near Stowmarket, offers borders as good as any. The house has the inestimable virtue of having remained in the Tollemache family for its entire life of five centuries. It was built in 1480 but little trace remains of the gardens of the past. The present owners are responsible for the splendid herbaceous borders that flank the approach to fine wrought iron gates. There are modern reconstructions of other old garden features at

Helmingham: the knot and herb gardens are less than twenty years old but are largely stocked with ancient plants and serve as a reminder of the exquisite simplicity of single flowers and of varieties that haven't fallen into the hands of breeders and 'improvers'.

Herbaceous borders feature also at Blickling Hall near Norwich, where four large rectangular herbaceous plantings are surrounded by rose beds. At the centre of the planting is as fine a focal point as you will find anywhere: a seventeenth-century fountain. This is a garden that has seen many changes and reinforces the point that gardens do and should evolve, for the present disposition of beds dates from between the wars, when Mrs Norah Lindsay remodelled a sunken Victorian garden of many smaller beds and topiary. I'm not sure that Mrs Lindsay has ever really received the credit she merits for her role in shaping the characteristic features of twentieth-century English gardens. She played a significant, but overlooked, part at several other important gardens and worked closely with Lawrence Johnston at Hidcote in Gloucestershire. Even so, her 1930s planting at Blickling was an evolution from an earlier Jacobean garden.

I've described how house and garden may or may not blend (see page 33), but Blickling reveals another garden feature, only realisable where there is space. Instead of relating the building entirely to the house, it can be planned instead around another, smaller building within the grounds. At Blickling, that building is the Temple, which may well be the work of William Kent, the early eighteenth-century designer. It was probably moved from its original position in the early nineteenth century. But it's the walk to the Temple during May that is one of my enduring memories of Blickling, for I know of few other shrub and tree plantings where flowers and foliage have been blended so superbly. Then the vivid hues of billowing banks of rhododendrons and azaleas in oranges, reds and yellows are set against a wonderful backdrop of the fresh young shoots of beech and yew.

But if the gardens at Helmingham recreate something older, and those at Blickling demonstrate garden evolution, those at Ickworth are an equally fine example of the way that English gardens have embraced the gardening traditions, not only of other times but also of other places. The house was built in the late eighteenth century by the Fourth Earl of Bristol, a man who loved things Italian. So the house is Italianate with a huge and imposing rotunda, curved wings, pavilions and a pillared portico. And the garden blends with it, and indeed serves it. For almost wherever you go in the garden, a vista opens up to take your eye back to the rotunda and the house. It is a wooded garden, heavy with evergreens, box, holm oak, cedars and yew, although a splendid *Koelreuteria paniculata* offers contrasting golden blossom in late summer. Like most good gardens, Ickworth also offers surprises; although in one case it is a surprise that perhaps shouldn't have happened. Tucked amongst the trees are gardens of gold- and silver-foliage plants, and what a welcome change they make to the white gardens that have become so thick on the ground of late. The Silver Garden includes not only interesting plants but also large lumps of rock that look very familiar. And so they are, for their rightful home is on the Giant's Causeway in Antrim, Northern Ireland. The Fourth Earl of Bristol, of course, was also Bishop of Derry. This can't be a coincidence.

Waterwise measures in the garden

What are the best plants to attract butterflies into my garden?

There are two aspects to this question, for it's one thing to attract butterflies; that's fairly easy. It requires rather more thought and is really more important to persuade them to remain. Plants to attract butterflies are those with nectar that they find especially appealing. I've given a short list of the most important, including of course, the best of all, the so-called butterfly bush itself, *Buddleja davidii*.

But to persuade them to remain, you must also supply the food plants for their caterpillars and to be honest, these don't make nearly such good subjects as garden ornamentals. In fact, a good many are classed as weeds. I do hope that you can find room somewhere, however, for a few examples of those that have the widest appeal for butterflies and for moths. Stinging nettles top the

PLANTS DIFFER IN their ability to tolerate drought and in the periods of growth when they benefit most from additional watering. But it is important to appreciate one simple, basic rule of watering to avoid wasting resources, especially at times of water shortage. If, in general, you ensure that a plant has most water at the time it is producing those parts that are the reason for its cultivation, then you will not go far wrong. So water flowers at flowering time, fruit trees and bushes as the fruit are swelling,

RIGHT: *Although small tortoiseshell butterflies are readily attracted by flowers such as this* Sedum spectabile, *or ice plant, they require stinging nettles if they are to breed and multiply.*

list, providing food for many species, including small tortoiseshells, commas, painted ladies, red admirals and peacocks. Other valuable species include docks and sorrels, native grasses, the buckthorn, willows, hawthorn and birch.

Ornamental plants of especial value in attracting butterflies include:

Buddleja	Lavender
Candytuft	Lilac
Golden rod	Michaelmas daisy
Honeysuckle	Pinks
Ice plant	Sweet violet
Lady's smock	Thyme

and vegetables as the roots, heads, fruits or tubers are forming.

There are three approaches to economising on water use. First, re-use as much household water as possible. Second, be efficient in your use of tap water. And third, store rainwater until you need to use it. Pretty well all once-used domestic water can find a role in the garden. The only exception is water that has had any form of bleach added, and I am also wary of the outpourings of dishwashers which use less than gentle detergents. And I should also add that I wouldn't use domestic waste water containing soaps or other materials on very young seedlings. Even a small quantity of dissolved matter can cause harm to tender

seedlings, but mature plants in the open garden should be perfectly safe.

Another point to remember is that water used directly from the mains should never be allowed to pour onto the garden through sprinklers unless there is some kind of cut-off device attached to the tap. Several companies now manufacture such equipment. At one end of the scale, these are simple valves that shut off after a given volume of water has been delivered or after a certain time has elapsed. At the other, they are rather sophisticated watering 'computers' that enable on and off periods to be programmed in advance. But I'm still amazed at the amount of water wasted by inappropriate equipment at the nozzle end of the hose-pipe. For far too many gardeners, a sprinkler is a sprinkler and they give no consideration to the choice of sprinkler or to the size and shape of the area being watered. Many modern sprinklers are adjustable in at least one of these respects and importantly so, for spraying water onto plants that have no particular requirement for it or, even worse, over the fence and onto your neighbour's garden, is no use to anyone.

And in passing, I should ask that no-one takes a leaf out of farmers' books. My own village is surrounded by farms with vast agricultural water-distributing apparatus that throws the stuff across roads and footpaths and seems designed to irrigate a large part of Warwickshire.

One of the most valuable devices to attach to the business end of your hose-pipe is not however a sprinkler of any sort, but a seeping hose. These may be laid over the soil surface or,

How best can I obtain early season colour with bedding plants?

By definition, annuals pass through their entire life cycle, from seed to seed, within a single season. They need to be pretty fast-growing therefore if they are to give much of a display in the spring in which they are sown. But there are ways to help them. The best and easiest method, but only with hardy annuals, is to sow them in the previous autumn. You can do this either directly into the open ground, or, better, into pots or trays kept over winter in a cold frame or cold greenhouse. Planted out in the spring, these will have a head start.

Annuals can be supplemented usefully with biennials. These, also by definition, are sown in one year to flower in the next and as they are sown in the early summer for transplanting to their flowering positions in the autumn, they will be even more advanced than autumn-sown annuals by the time spring arrives. The only serious drawback is that there are very few suitable biennial flowers, but never underestimate the value of the two commonest, wallflowers and sweet williams.

Two main types of wallflower are grown in gardens, the common wallflower, *Erysimum cheiri* and the Siberian wallflower, *Erysimum hieracliifolium*. Depending on the varieties chosen, flowering will be from April through to June. The common wallflower is grown by the million for planting in municipal parks and gardens and, if you simply ask for wall-flowers, this is the one you will be sold.

Once there were dozens of varieties in a very wide range of colours. These have been reduced significantly over the years although there are still varieties in each of the three groups: Intermediates which grow to approximately 40-45cm, Dwarf Bedding types, (usually given the name 'Bedder') which attain about 35cm, and the compact 'Tom Thumb' varieties which are especially useful for small areas, fronts of borders or for very windy sites where the early season gales can cause problems with large plants. The Siberian wallflower reaches approximately the same size as the Dwarf Bedding forms but is later flowering, tends to be grown more as a true perennial and is only available in gold and yellow.

Although they flower a little later than most wallflowers, sweet williams have long been cottage garden favourites for spring colour. They may be grown in the same way as wallflowers although being of more manageable size, quite conveniently can be sown initially in boxes. Most varieties reach 45-60cm and the auricula-eyed forms, with red or pink flowers and a white eye, are especially attractive.

better still, buried just below it. They use very little water but gently ooze water to saturate an area approximately 30cm wide on either side of the hosepipe. And my handy hint of the moment is to install one in your melon frame; the result is wonderfully succulent melons.

But not all water comes from the mains tap. Water originates in the clouds and the more that you can intercept before it becomes the property of the water company, the better and cheaper it will be. Any fairly small area of roof should have a gutter and downpipe system that enables you to collect the water that falls on it in a large barrel or butt. I do stress that it must be a fairly small area of roof, nonetheless. You may be tempted to collect water from the roof of your house but you will simply find that the butt fills and overflows in only a few minutes during rainy weather. I find it best to restrict your water collection in this way to the greenhouse, shed and perhaps garage.

Modern butts are made of plastic, with taps and removable covers; the more attractive, traditional ones, from wood. Do remember that rain water butts harbour a variety of wild life, including some organisms that cause plant disease. A useful maxim, therefore, is only to use collected rain water outdoors. In the warmth of the greenhouse, any harmful organisms will be able to incubate and cause trouble. And rain water shouldn't be stored in zinc-coated or iron vessels, as it will accumulate harmful metal residues.

Perhaps more people will be in the fortunate position, as I am, of having an underground water

Can you tell me how best to grow sweet peas?

Sweet peas like sunshine, so always choose a site with a good depth of top-soil and good drainage, that affords them as much light and air as possible, and avoid any position overhung by trees or shaded by buildings.

Prepare the soil as early as possible, preferably in the autumn. Dig in well-rotted compost or farmyard manure to a depth of 45-60cm and add two good handfuls of bone meal per square metre. Allow about 60cm width for each row of plants and a circle of about 60cm diameter if they are to be grown in clumps.

There are several different methods of raising plants. The seed may be sown outdoors in the autumn; sown in pots or boxes in the autumn and overwintered in a cold frame for spring-planting; sown under protection in the early spring for transplanting later; or sown directly into the garden in April. The latter is generally the least satisfactory and should really be a last resort. Autumn-sowing into pots is my recommendation, with spring-sowing under protection as second choice generally, but advisable as a first option in the North.

For an autumn sowing, I use a soil-based seedling compost. In early October, soak the seeds overnight and then sow two to each 7.5cm pot at a depth of 1-1.5cm. Water after sowing and place in the cold frame. Once the seedlings have emerged, leave the frame covers off in all except the very wettest or very coldest winter weather. After they have produced two or three pairs of leaves, pinch out the tops to encourage bushy growth. Germination of dark-seeded varieties especially may be improved by nicking the seeds on the side opposite the eye with the tip of a sharp knife. Alternatively, soak all seed for at least 12 hours before sowing.

Sweet peas may be planted out in most areas of the country towards the end of March; allow a space of about 20cm between each plant. There are several ways in which the plants may be supported; exhibition growers use a semi-permanent framework of posts, but 2.5m long bamboo canes, either in a double row or a tripod group for clumps of plants, are the most popular.

Nonetheless, for simple garden culture within a mixed border, sweet peas can look very effective simply allowed to scramble at random up twiggy branches or a tall wigwam of bamboo canes. Allow one cane or branch per plant.

storage chamber. I have two and they were installed sometime in the nineteenth century to obtain soft water for washing. Similar reservoirs were often built beneath large greenhouses. But why, oh why, are such things not built today? If anyone is doing construction work around their house, or even having a house built, I would ask that your builder looks seriously at installing a vaulted, brick-lined chamber under a patio to hold rainwater draining off the roof. I think storage chambers are due for a come-back.

The pine

IT'S HARD TO BELIEVE that all of our commonest conifers are alien and that there are only three native conifers in Britain. The Scots pine, the yew and the juniper are all that we possess. We did once have more: the Norway spruce (Christmas tree to most people) and the Silver fir at least lived here before the last Ice Age but never made it back again when the ice retreated. But the extensive planting of exotic species for forestry within recent history has given us a distorted view of things. Even that glorious tree, the larch, which hails from much of continental Europe has never been a British native, while the most widely planted of all, and one that covers vast tracts of upland country, is a plant whose natural home is a narrow coastal strip from Alaska down to central California. Yes, if you live in Kielder in Northumbria, I'm sure that *Picea sitchensis*, the Sitka spruce, must be synonymous with the word conifer.

Can you give some ideas for quick-growing flowers for a child's garden?

I like to let children have their own small garden where, under supervision, they can experiment with almost anything that they choose. Nonetheless, the one virtue that most young children lack is patience and they become bored very quickly. So guide them towards trying plants that grow quickly and give dramatic results. This is where some of the annuals come into their own. Few grow as quickly or as dramatically as sunflowers do, but you must exercise supervision in the number of seeds that are

In East Anglia, you may also get a distorted view of the relative importance of different trees, but at least those that crowd in on all sides as you drive across Thetford chase are from closer to home. For the predominant trees there are pines. Some are native Scots pine, *Pinus sylvestris*, others the blacker barked Austrian pine, *Pinus nigra*. Even so, these plantation trees bear little resemblance to the way that native Scots pines should appear. Cultivated pines are tall, slender trees, much beloved of foresters but distinctly lacking in character. It just isn't natural for us in Britain to think of pines as massive, twisted and gnarled, in the way that ancient oaks are massive, twisted and gnarled and yet that is the source of their real beauty.

Nonetheless, neither in ancient nor in modern forms are *Pinus nigra* and *Pinus sylvestris* the best of garden trees. Until they are very old, or at least

sown; a dozen or more sunflowers can leave very little room for anything else. Another good quick-growing choice is borage, a big bushy annual herb that, once established, will self-sow for years and has masses of star-shaped flowers in electric blue. Among smaller growing species, calendula or pot marigold can always be relied on, together with nasturtium, nigella (love-in-a-mist), nemesia and, for something different, annual hibiscus, the flower-of-an-hour, which, as its name suggests, has very short-lived individual flowers but blooms over a long period. It also produces very attractive inflated seed pods. By and large, especially for young children, choose plants with fairly large seeds that can be sown directly into their flowering positions. There will be plenty of time later for children to be introduced to seed boxes and pricking out.

planted in vast numbers, I find they offer rather little ornamental appeal. Clearly not all gardeners feel the same for they have both received the Royal Horticultural Society's coveted Award of Garden Merit. But in disagreeing about these two, I don't want to suggest that gardeners shouldn't grow pines in general. On the contrary, I feel that if more people knew more about the scope that the genus offers, these fine plants could grace a far greater number of gardens, big and small. They are undemanding, easy to establish and easy to care for and suffer from few of the pest and diseases problems that plague many popular trees.

All pines are trees, not shrubs, but small or dwarf varieties do exist among many species and I think that it is with them that gardeners should begin, and then progress to the larger varieties and species if space permits.

Pines can be subdivided on the basis of the number of needles in each cluster – two, three or five. Generally, the more the needles and the longer the needles, the more attractive the plant.

The following short list is based on those dwarf forms that I have grown personally. Most will attain a size of about 60 x 60cm, will thrive in most soils and most areas and the majority have received the prestigious Award of Garden Merit from the Royal Horticultural Society:

P. contorta (two-needled). The lodgepole pine from the Rocky Mountains is a most unattractive plant when a full-sized tree and fairly widely planted for timber in exposed areas. The dwarf form 'Frisian Gold', with golden yellow foliage and irregularly rounded form, is quietly very attractive.

P. heldreichii leucodermis (two-needled). The Bosnian pine is a rather attractive, shapely tree with blue cones, although too big for most gardens. Its smaller form 'Schmidtii', which is dark green and irregularly rounded, is a lovely plant.

P. mugo (two-needled). The European mountain pine is never a very big tree and has several attractive dwarf forms of which 'Mops', rather bright green and irregularly rounded, is easily the best.

P. strobus (five-needled). The North American Weymouth pine isn't planted in its full-sized form as it is prone to serious rust disease, but the long needles lend themselves beautifully to the dwarf habit of two lovely varieties, 'Radiata' and 'Reinshaus', both bluish-green, irregularly rounded and delightful; they just ask to be stroked.

If your garden is large enough and you want to move up to full-sized pines, I suggest that you begin with the longest needled hardy species that you can find. The Mexican *Pinus montezumae* would be top of my list, followed closely by the Himalayan Bhutan pine, *Pinus wallichiana* and, in milder areas, the Mexican white pine *Pinus ayacahuite*. There is also a fine hybrid between the Bhutan and Mexican white pine called *Pinus holfordiana* which in its best forms combines the virtues of both.

Can you recommend a range of annuals that can be grown to dry for flower arrangements?

If you are careful enough and know what you are doing, it's possible to dry almost any type of flower. Some are undoubtedly difficult to dry. For a start choose those that don't have very fleshy or soft petals and that can be tied into bunches and hung up to air dry. There is a group of mainly South African annuals, some of which are often called everlasting flowers, that is particularly satisfactory. Most are characterised by bright, cheerful daisy-like flowers and rather papery bracts. Some of the annual grasses also make excellent dried flowers.

Here are some annual flowers suitable for air-drying for flower arrangements:

Looking after the soil

EVEN THE MOST experienced of gardeners sometimes take their soil for granted. It's the single most important feature of your garden and yet it just isn't accorded the respect that it deserves. And nowhere is this more true than if you garden on a light free-draining soil such as in the Suffolk coastal

RIGHT: *Helichrysums are among the most familiar (and vivid) of the annuals that can be grown for drying and so be appreciated all year round.*

Briza maxima (Quaking grass). Dangling, purple-green ribbed flower heads. 45cm/18in.

Clarkia amoena. Double or semi-double flowers like small azaleas in white, red, pink or purple. 60cm/24in.

Delphinium consolida (Larkspur). Miniature delphiniums with spikes of white, pink, red or blue flowers. Depending on variety, 30cm/12in to 1m/40 in or more.

Helichrysum bracteatum (Straw flower). Double flowers with straw-like rays in white, pink, purple, yellow or orange. 30cm/12in dwarf types or 1m/40in tall types.

Helipterum roseum (Everlasting flower). Single or double daisy flowers in white or pink. 35cm/14in.

Iberis (Candytuft). Double flowers with rather flat heads in white, pink or red. 25-45cm/10-18in.

Lagurus (Hare's tail grass). Fluffy white, cottony flower heads. 45cm/18in.

Nigella (Love-in-a-mist). Button-like flower heads in white, red, pink or blue surrounded by feather foliage. 45cm/18in.

Osteospermum (Star of the veldt). Single or semi-double daisy flowers with dark eyes and white, yellow, orange or pink rays. 30cm/12in.

Salvia. Spikes of elongated, tubular flowers in red, pink or purple. 30-45cm/12-18in.

Scabious. Neat, button-like heads of white, blue, pink or purple flowers. Depending on variety, 45cm/18in or about 1m/40in.

area. Rainwater drains through it at great speed, taking away nutrients as it does so. And it's people attempting to garden on this type of soil who most frequently enquire about the relative merits of fertilisers on the one hand and the different types of manure or compost on the other. "Which is best for my soil?" they ask me. I find myself having to explain that the two are quite different in composition and function; and that you need them both.

Fertilisers are plant foods. Their purpose is to supplement the nutrients naturally present in the soil. The reason they are needed is because, in gardening, we place much greater demands on the soil's reserves than happens in nature. We expect our plants to be bigger, more lush and generally better yielding. And this is true whether the yield is measured in fruit, vegetables or flowers. In the vegetable garden, and to some extent the annual flower garden, we also repeatedly crop the same area of soil. At the end of the season, one year's plants are uprooted and discarded, soon to be replaced by next year's newcomers. This just doesn't happen in the wild. Plants slowly die down, rot in situ and then, gradually, as a result of seed germination, a new batch emerges. In rushing things along, we quite simply put a strain on our soil and this is why fertilisers are needed.

It doesn't matter in which form you apply plant food. Whether supplied as organic fertilisers or artificials, the basic plant nutrients of nitrogen, phosphate, potash and other chemicals are what matter and they must break down in the soil into these simple units before plants can absorb them. I think it's with organic fertilisers however that the confusion with composts arises; if for no other reason than that composts are one form of what is often called organic matter. Organic fertilisers originated in some once-living organism, plant or animal. Their names generally indicate this: dried

I have a rather shady spot and wonder what herbaceous perennials will fare best here?

The ability of many herbaceous perennials to tolerate shade is an important aspect of mixed border design, for the taller-growing inhabitants of the border will inevitably take some light from the lower-growing ones. In a naturally shady situation therefore, it's perfectly possible to select and plant simply those that are happy in such conditions. However, it must be appreciated that the range of colour and form will be very much more limited than in the ideal position for a mixed border, which is with maximum exposure to the sun. The following list gives some suggestions for shade-tolerant herbaceous perennials, although it should be remembered that, in a modern mixed border, some shade-tolerant shrubs will be needed also.

Aconitum

Alchemilla

Aruncus

Asarum

Astilbe

Cimicifuga

Digitalis

Euphorbia
  (*E. cyparissias*,
  E. robbiae)

Filipendula
  (Cultivated forms
  of *F. ulmaria*)

Geranium
  (*G. phaeum*,
  G. maculatum,
  G. macrorrhizum)

Hellebore

Omphalodes

Trachystemon

blood, fish meal, hoof and horn, bone meal, guano. They have all been refined before they fall into the use of gardeners.

Organic matter however is much cruder stuff. It too originated in living things, but has been little refined since. It includes animal manures, garden compost and mushroom compost. Of course, they also contain basic plant nutrients but because they are much more bulky and unrefined, the proportions of nutrients are much less. Take a few examples: dried blood contains 10-13 % nitrogen, fish meal 6-10% nitrogen, bone meal about 24% phosphate and 4% nitrogen. The commonly used mixture, fish, blood and bone contains nitrogen, phosphate and potash in the approximate ratios of 5.1% nitrogen, 5% phosphate and 6.5% potash while its artificial fertiliser equivalent, Growmore, contains about 7% each nitrogen, phosphate and potash. Compare these with farmyard manure or good garden compost which contain only about 0.25% of each.

It's clear you will need a pretty huge dose of compost to give your plants as much food as they will obtain from a handful of fertiliser. To grow cabbages successfully, would take 4 kilograms of pig manure per square metre of plot, if they aren't given additional fertiliser. I don't want to give the impression that organic matter, bulky organic matter, isn't important. Its value and role comes in improving the structure of soil; of helping to break down a clay like that so familiar to London gardeners, or build up a free-draining sandy soil as in much of East Anglia. So to return to the question, "Which is best for my soil?", the answer is that bulky organic matter is directly of most value to the soil, and so indirectly to plants; for plants will grow best if they are in good, well-tended ground. Fertilisers by contrast have no indirect effect. Their value is direct, as essential plant nutrients. The good gardener uses both.

THE
KITCHEN
GARDEN

*The Welsh Borders contain
some of the finest agricultural land in
Britain. Those deep, rich soils have
yielded the grass on which Hereford
cattle were raised but they have also
given rise to a relatively little known crop
of fine gardens, in which grow some
of the country's very best fruit
and vegetables.*

Fruit for a small garden

MOST GARDENERS ENJOY growing fruit and vegetables, and in naturally fertile areas such as Herefordshire and the Welsh borders and the Fenlands of Lincolnshire, the rewards of a kitchen garden are abundant.

Small may be beautiful, I'm not really sure; but when it comes to fruit trees, there's no denying that it's extremely useful. Not so many years ago, planting a fruit tree meant two things: a fairly long wait before you obtained any fruit, and then an investment in a ladder in order to be able to pick the crop. And if you had a small garden, you could almost forget about tree fruit; a single apple, pear or plum tree would dwarf your plot.

Today, everyone can grow fruit and benefit from the wonderful range of varieties available. Three things have made this possible. First, the advent of rootstocks that exercise a size-limiting effect on any variety grafted on them. Second, in a few instances, the introduction of varieties with significantly less vigour. And third, the use of training and pruning techniques that produce smaller trees.

It is in the soft fruit garden that the choice of variety and of training method are all-important. For raspberries, select those varieties such as 'Glen Moy' or 'Glen Prosen' that have limited vigour and upright canes. Avoid the widely arching types such as 'Malling Joy'. Blackberries and hybrid berries are a little trickier, for most are fairly vigorous. My experience suggests that your best selection and most manageable plants will come from 'Medana Tayberry', 'Loch Ness' blackberry, and 'LY 654' thornless loganberry. Train them as fans against a wall or, if you have one, against one side of your fruit cage. Among redcurrants, whitecurrants and gooseberries,

PREVIOUS PAGE: *Not many places blend trees and ornamental plantings so effectively as Hergest Croft, seen here as the beauty of spring unfolds.*

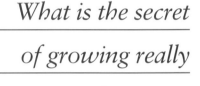

What is the secret of growing really good carrots?

In horticultural shows, carrots are '20-point' vegetables, up to 20 points being awarded in their class. No other vegetable scores more than this and it's a fair indication that they aren't among the easiest to grow. But the difficulty really lies in two areas only: the soil and the control of the carrot fly.

The soil must permit those long roots to grow unimpeded. It must be, therefore, light, free-draining and free from stones, hard clods or an impervious layer several centimetres below the surface. If any of these are incorrect, the roots will become twisted and forked or fanged. So it's well worth taking extra care in the preparation of the carrot

vigour is less variable, and less important too, for you should simply grow your chosen varieties as cordons; single, double or triple depending on the space available. Blackcurrants alone, among soft fruit, boast a variety bred specially for limited space. 'Ben Sarek' is a wonderful, high-yielding, compact, mid-season blackcurrant for gardens; two plants should satisfy even the most besotted blackcurrant grower.

Among tree fruit, there has always been a great deal of variation in vigour. As I write, I have my kitchen garden in view and can look down the tunnel of apples and see that while the most vigorous, the two 'Golden Delicious' trees, long ago reached the top of the tunnel from either side, at the other end of the scale, poor old 'Pitmaston Pineapple' is only halfway up. But it's the use of the rootstocks bred in this country during the present century at the old John Innes Institute and, later, the East Malling Research Institute, that has been of revolutionary and quite extraordinary benefit. This was achieved by careful selection and breeding of plants that would ultimately only be used for the value of their roots; a remarkable state of affairs, without parallel in plant breeding.

The mechanism by which the roots of a plant can exercise an effect on any variety (any variety may it be noted), that is grafted onto it, is through some process involving plant hormones. But when you are choosing these plants for your own garden, be aware that there are limits to what can be achieved. Remember my observation on my tunnel of apple trees. All of these trees are on the same rootstock, M 26, and yet some trees are bigger than the others. You have to imagine a tug of war between rootstock and fruiting variety. A dwarfing rootstock can diminish the vigour of a robust variety and by the same token, a more vigorous

bed. Applying fresh manure to the ground too soon before sowing will also cause fanging. The fresh manure applied for the preceding crop will be sufficient.

Controlling carrot fly with insecticides has never been effective. It's much better to try to dissuade the female fly from reaching the plants. Horticultural mesh may be used to cover the carrot bed or a 'fence' or barrier of plastic sheet around 60cm high erected around the plants. The operation of the barrier depends on the fact that the insect flies close to the ground and so is deterred on the barrage balloon principle. Always sow carrots sparsely to avoid the need for thinning out the plants later as every disturbance of the foliage releases an aroma attractive to the flies. If you do have to thin out the plants, always water them afterwards to deaden the smell. But finally, I would suggest that you try the varieties 'Sytan' or even better 'Fly Away', which have considerable resistance to the fly.

rootstock can give a kick up the backside to a rather feeble one. If I had grown 'Pitmaston Pineapple' on something rather more vigorous such as MM 106, it would have been closer now in size to the 'Golden Delicious'.

And when you are choosing and growing dwarf trees in your own garden, remember too the relationship between the rootstock and the soil. A dwarfing rootstock, especially the very dwarfing M 27, must have good growing conditions. It's ideal indeed for growing in a container in high quality John Innes soil-based potting compost. By contrast, if you have naturally poor soil in your garden, or very cold, exposed conditions, you must use a more vigorous, tougher rootstock.

The benefits of size-limiting rootstocks have not been as great with other fruits. However, if you choose pears grafted onto 'Quince A' or, on poorer soils, 'Quince C', and plums on 'Pixy', your trees at least will be manageable. I mentioned earlier, however, the difference in vigour between different fruit tree varieties and in recent years there has been one notable success in bringing a fruit within reach, quite literally, of more gardeners. I remember the cherry trees that we had in the garden when I was a boy. They were huge. Not only did you need a ladder to pick the fruit, and several trees to effect pollination, you found yourself disturbing entire flocks of birds who had managed to reach them first. That has changed in two ways. We now have a reliable, less vigorous rootstock for cherries in the shape of 'Colt'. And the second leap forward came with the relatively non-vigorous but self-fertile variety 'Stella'. The combination of 'Colt' and 'Stella' has been a benefit indeed.

Are Oriental leafy vegetables very successful in our climate?

This question is a common one and stems from older gardeners or those with longer memories. The first of the Oriental vegetables to appear in our seed catalogues some years ago was the Chinese cabbage (sometimes called Chinese leaves). Almost invariably, these bolted or ran to seed and so proved a disappointment. The problems arose because bolting can be triggered by a combination of relatively low temperatures and long days; exactly the conditions of the early British summer. To some extent, the problem is overcome by not sowing outdoors before mid-summer, but new bolt-resistant varieties of Chinese cabbage and a range of other Oriental crops are now available.

I confess that I find some Oriental vegetables tough and tasteless, while others seem abnormally prone to flea beetle and other pest attack. The following is a list of those that have given me most success:

RIGHT: *Not all Oriental vegetables are suitable for British gardens although Pak choi is one of the more popular and reliable.*

Chinese cabbage. Many types, including loose leafy forms and barrel heads (rather like cos lettuce). Sow after mid-summer; need late season protection. New varieties constantly being introduced.

Chrysanthemum greens. Variety of ornamental chrysanthemum. Best as autumn green crop; young leaves in salads, older leaves cooked.

Komatsuna. Best are the very hardy varieties grown as winter greens for cooking. Imagine a cross between spring cabbage and spinach in flavour.

Mibuna. Useful as autumn/early winter greens. Mild mustard flavour; use cooked.

Mizuna. Attractive dark green leaves with white stalks. Good 'cut and come again' plants for autumn; best cooked.

Mustards. Useful as winter greens, although ideally with some protection. Unreliable for summer because of bolting. Some very attractive purple leaved varieties, although they can make large plants.

Pak choi. Similar to Chinese cabbage with broad leaf mid-ribs. Choose bolt-resistant varieties or sow after midsummer.

Radishes. Red and green fleshed varieties; rather more astringent than western radishes. Choose bolt-resistant types or sow after midsummer.

More recently still, 'Stella' has been joined by other self-fertile cherries in 'Sunburst' and 'Lapins' and, most interestingly, by an even less vigorous form called 'Stella Compact'.

Quite clearly, the story hasn't ended yet and I have every confidence that more neat, compact fruit trees will emerge in years to come. The miniature orchard is almost with us and, as far as cherries are concerned, this might mean that competition with birds is a thing of the past because small trees can be netted or grown in a cage, just as soft fruit are already.

Growing tasty tomatoes

MOST PEOPLE OWN greenhouses to grow tomatoes. I know, in fact, that many people own greenhouses for no other purpose and it saddens me to see them lying empty once the year's crop has been cleared away. But there's no denying that the tomato is a quite essential part of our gardening season and whether it is grown in the protection of a greenhouse, outdoors in milder areas or even, with the modern miniature varieties, on window ledges or in hanging baskets, summer wouldn't be summer without it. But it wasn't always so. Tomatoes are relatively new to British gardens.

Is there a way to prevent my onions from going mouldy?

Onions generally go mouldy for one of two reasons: spring or salad onions because they have been affected by a disease called white rot, and bulb onions in store, because of a disease called neck rot. White rot can't effectively be controlled and once you see the symptoms of yellowing leaves and a white, fluffy mould at the base of the plant, my advice is to select a small area to use specifically for onions. Construct

The natural home of *Lycopersicon*, the tomato, is in western South America, especially in the foothills of the Andes where seven different species occur. They are rambling, scrambling plants, more or less perennial and often to be found in rather rocky inhospitable conditions. The most important is *Lycopersicon esculentum*. The wild plant has yellow flowers and fruit that are variable in size and colour, ranging from yellow through orange to red. The European explorers to South America in the sixteenth century soon discovered them but they were considered at worst poisonous, and at best aphrodisiac. It was for the latter reason that they were brought back to Europe, apparently first to Italy. For many years, they were called *pomo d'oro* (golden apples), love apples or Peruvian apples. The name tomato came later, in the seventeenth century from the Spanish *tomate*, which came in turn from a South American Indian word. They had certainly reached England by 1595 but it was some time before people became bold enough to eat them. This was quite understandable for they belong to a family, the Solanaceae, that includes some of the most poisonous of all plants and it remains a mystery how and why the edible nature of tomatoes, potatoes and aubergines came to light.

Lycopersicon esculentum is a variable plant and once gardeners began to grow it and, even more significantly, plant breeders took it into their laboratories, some of this variation was immediately capitalised upon. For some reason, the red-fruited forms were selected in preference to the golden, although a number of varieties with yellow or golden fruits are still available. They tend to have foliage more like that of their close relative, the potato. Large-fruited 'beefsteak' tomatoes have gained favour in warmer parts of the world where they can be easily cultivated outdoors. The variety *L. esculentum cerasiforme*, the cherry tomato, has given rise to some garden varieties, most especially the small-fruited, very sweet-tasting forms such as 'Gardeners' Delight' while the variety *L. esculentum pimpinellifolium*, the currant tomato, has yielded the even smaller, but somewhat bland tomatoes seen in the salads of smart restaurants. The variety *L. esculentum pyriforme* with pear-shaped fruit has also been used to produce a number of attractively fruited forms, both red and yellow, although these are seldom seen in gardens.

Regardless of their fruit type however, tomato varieties can be placed in two groups: the cordon, upright or indeterminate varieties and the bush or determinate types. The former, including my favourite 'Gardeners' Delight',

a raised bed with planks and fill this with soil from part of the garden that has never grown onions. Forget about crop rotation, as the white rot fungus can survive for over 20 years, and keep your onions in this one bed. It's even worth keeping a spare set of tools specially for use in this area to avoid bringing in the disease with contaminated soil.

Neck rot is a bluish mould on the onion bulb, but it only occurs in store. It is much easier to control but by an unexpected method. The neck rot fungus doesn't as a rule infect the growing plant; it is present on the seed or on the set at the time of planting or sowing. Dust onion seed routinely, therefore, with the fungicide carbendazim or soak onion sets in a spray-strength mixture of carbendazim for half an hour before planting.

Could you give me some ideas please for a simple herb garden?

Every garden should have some herbs. Every cook needs them and even the tiniest plot will be enhanced by their ornamental value. Given limited space, however, I would confine myself to those that have at least some culinary value and attempt to select the most attractive varieties among them. Their requirements are fairly straightforward. Almost all herbs need a sunny position and few will tolerate heavy cold soil. If your garden is naturally heavy, then grow a small selection in containers with a soil-based potting compost. Mint, because of its propensity to spread, is always best confined in a container, even if this is sunk in the soil of the bed itself. Apart from the annual/biennial types such as basil and parsley, don't raise herbs from seed. The best varieties don't come true and you will fare much better by buying small plants and either renewing them by taking cuttings every three years or buying fresh stock.

are deliberately trained to form a single stem, the side-branches that arise adjacent to the leaves being pinched out. This is called 'side-shooting'. By contrast, the bush varieties, among which 'The Amateur' is excellent, are allowed to branch and form a mound of growth, much like that of their wild ancestors, although rather more luxuriantly.

Because garden tomatoes are raised from seed, it's not often realised that they can be grown from cuttings and can also be grafted. The latter has been a particularly useful technique where tomatoes were grown in soil contaminated with eelworm, wilt or other root diseases. Rootstocks resistant to these problems were used and normal fruiting varieties grafted onto them. The resistant rootstock may still be obtained but its use has declined with the development of growing techniques that don't use soil. For many years, commercial tomato crops were grown in prepared composts, either soil-based or more recently soil-less. These remain popular in gardens where growing bags of soil-less mixtures or, best of all, bottomless ring culture pots of soil-based compost standing on a gravel bed are extensively used. In commerce, most tomatoes

Allium sativum (Garlic). Use green shoots for flavouring.

Allium schoenoprasum (Chives)

Anthriscus cerefolium (Chervil)

Artemisia dracunculus (French tarragon). Note, not the coarse Russian variety.

Helichrysum italicum (Curry plant)

Laurus nobilis (Sweet bay). Grow as a miniature shrub.

Mentha suaveolens (Apple mint)

Melissa officinalis 'Aurea' (Variegated lemon balm)

Ocimum basilicum (Basil). Annual, sow in spring.

Origanum vulgare 'Aureum' (Golden Oregano)

Petroselinum crispum 'Moss Curled' (Parsley). Biennial; sow in spring and autumn.

Rosmarinus officinalis 'Miss Jessopp's Upright' (Rosemary). Clip to keep neat and compact shape.

Salvia officinalis 'Tricolor' (Variegated sage)

Thymus vulgaris 'Silver Posie' (Variegated thyme)

ABOVE: *It used to be said that plum tomatoes weren't successful but improved varieties have changed that in recent years.*

are now grown in conditions that utilise neither soil nor compost, but comprise an inert medium in which the roots are anchored and in which they are constantly bathed by a gently moving current of liquid fertiliser. A far cry from the rocky foothills of their homeland.

Great gardens of the Welsh borders

OFFA, THE EIGHTH-CENTURY King of Mercia, knew a thing or two about building to last. He left the most enduring legacy of earth-moving along the Welsh Borders in his celebrated fortification know as Offa's Dyke. I rather doubt if he had much time for gardening. Other residents of the region certainly have and it is an area with some hauntingly lovely gardens. Yet many are evidently secret for I know of no other part of the British Isles in which there are so many fine gardens, close to centres of population and yet so relatively little known.

I have friends who consider Hergest Croft the finest garden in England although it is absent, mystifyingly, from some garden guide books. Perhaps this is because it is thought of by some as an arboretum rather than a garden, for it's unarguably one of the finest collections of trees and shrubs in private hands. It is large by any standard for a private property; but then you do need 20 hectares to accommodate several thousand species and include one each of the National Collections of maples and birches and the sole collection of zelkovas, those interesting relatives of the elms.

Hergest Croft lies to the north of Hereford and has been in the same family for four generations. The garden is one hundred years old, its cre-

Can you recommend ways of storing fresh fruit successfully?

Apples and pears are the only garden fruits that can be stored fresh, straight after harvesting, for more than a few days. Plums, other stone fruits like cherries and peaches, and all soft fruit, soon deteriorate and should be stored frozen, made into jams or preserves or, a favourite with me, bottled. But even with such relatively tough fruits as apples, some care is needed if they are to last for an appreciable time. It's important to choose the most suitable varieties, both culinary and dessert. Generally, the early-maturing varieties will not store and should be used straight from the tree. They soon become soft and the flesh turns fluffy and tasteless.

Pick fruit for storage with care. Never use windfalls, never use any from which the stalk has been pulled and never use any that have small wounds, bruises or signs of pest or disease damage. After much trial and error, I now use one of two methods of storing. I either arrange the fruit singly, but not touching, on slatted racks or in slatted trays; or I store them in bags. The bags should be clear plastic, new and unused and about ten fruit placed in each. I tie the tops loosely and punch several holes in each bag for ventilation. The bags are also placed on shelves. Pears need checking regularly for ripeness after they have been picked and for this reason they are best kept apart from apples which won't benefit from the constant disturbance.

Ideally, a small shed or part of a larger one should be set aside for the purpose but the main requirements of any storage place are that it should have as uniform a temperature as possible, be frost-free and not subject (as garages are) to smells of paint or petrol.

ation beginning in 1896 with the banker William Banks. There was little to go on except for some existing, relatively mature trees, but there was a good climate and a good soil. The soil, rich and acidic, is of immense importance. You can't grow good trees and shrubs anywhere on shallow soil but the acidity and shelter mean that Hergest Croft is host to the finest collection of rhododendrons that I know in any British garden away from the west coast. The rhododendrons are big and spectacular but whilst they, of course, require the acid conditions, other trees and shrubs, those that simply benefit from them, are spectacular too. Birches, in general, are better in slight acidity and it's no surprise that a National Collection is here, with particularly beautiful examples of some of the white-barked and puzzlingly similar Himalayan species such as *Betula jacquemontii*. Acers, too, give of their best in rich, slightly acid soil and the range of species here is particularly fine, indeed, apart from the varieties of *Acer palmatum* and *Acer japonicum*, it's all but comprehensive. The fact that the trees and shrubs are enhanced by borders is what justifies my considering Hergest Croft a 'proper' garden and once you tire of the trees, there's a Victorian kitchen garden and roses to take your interest.

Hodnet Hall in Shropshire is a curious red brick house of 1870, built in the Elizabethan style. But there is nothing curious about its gardens, begun in 1922 by Brigadier Algernon Heber-Percy, father of the present owner. Unless, that is, you consider owning one of the largest water gardens in the country to be curious. And unless it is curious to take on the gardening of over 24 hectares by making vast and complex plantings. The reasons for the creation of the gardens of Hodnet were a mixture of indulgence and pragmatism. Heber-Percy had always been a keen and enthusiastic gardener and decided to let his ambitions run riot. But he was also a clear-headed enough businessman to realise that by attracting visitors, his gardens could pay their way and support the upkeep of his enormous house. It was visionary enough in the 1920s. The house has since been reduced to more manageable size but the gardens seem to have grown in proportion. Heber-Percy created his water gardens by damming a small stream which flowed down the valley (no, don't try it yourself; it's now illegal) and this has resulted in a succession of pools and water features. All have been planted with great intensity and imagination.

Burford House lies on the banks of the River Teme at Tenbury Wells in Worcestershire, about 16 kilometres downstream from Ludlow. When he bought the house, John Treasure acquired just 1.6 hectares of extensive lawn, a few specimen trees, an apple orchard and meadow land. The secret of Burford House Gardens today is their deceptiveness. So many gardeners and garden designers strive to create the illusion of more space than is actually present; very few achieve it in the way that John Treasure did. The effect has arisen in a variety of ways.

The formal lawns, terrace, patio and pool of the south and west fronts of the property blend with complete harmony into the remaining

RIGHT: *The huge garden of Hergest Croft boasts one of the largest collections of trees in private hands; yet it is still more of a garden than an arboretum.*

informality. But there are several ways that this informally planted area of the garden could have been used to create the impression of space. Treasure, by and large, opted for the more difficult alternative of using a device that is one of the most misunderstood and inappropriately used in gardening, the island bed.

The island beds at Burford House are curved beds with projections and bays. They interlock and interweave visually to create, as in almost no other garden I know, a feeling of depth, an impression of many corners, around all of which must reside something worth seeing. The garden urges you to go on and on, without ever letting you know whether you are walking in straight lines or circles; and often fooling you into not knowing quite where all that water is.

My apples always contain maggots. How can I prevent this?

The maggots in apples are almost invariably the larvae of the codling moth, one of the commonest garden pests. The female moths fly into gardens in early summer and lay their eggs on the young fruits and the leaves. Within a couple of weeks, the caterpillars hatch and enter the young fruit, usually very close to the 'eye' so they aren't seen. Any direct action such as chemical spray therefore must be applied at a very critical time, after hatching but before

To rotate or not?

THAT DANGEROUS CONCEPT, 'conventional wisdom' is to blame. It says that every year, you must ensure that each type of vegetable is growing on a different part of the garden from that on which it grew last year. Gardening experts tend slavishly to give this advice, season after season, and gardeners tend, equally slavishly, to follow it. But over the years, I've come to realise that a good deal of the theory behind rotation really is theory and has little bearing on proper gardening.

There are, we are told, three principles behind rotation. First, different vegetables have different nutrient requirements. So by moving them around, you will ensure that a greater part of the nutrients naturally present in the soil are utilised; to put it simply, if, for instance, you grow a plant with a high potash demand this year, then you should grow one with a high phosphate demand next year. Second, given the break between plants of the same type and given the fact that many pests and disease fungi are fairly specific in

the fruit have been penetrated. This is all but impossible for not all caterpillars hatch at the same moment and in any event, effective spraying of large trees is impractical.

The best answer lies in using traps that contain a chemical that mimics the female insect's pheromone or sex attractant. Simple traps are available commercially and should be hung in the trees in late May, baited with the pheromone. The male codling moths fly into the traps where they are held by a sticky glue. Relatively few of the females are therefore fertilised and the number of caterpillars is significantly reduced. It's important to renew the sticky insert after about five weeks. A similar trap (but with a different pheromone) is available for a related pest, the plum moth.

the types of plant that they will attack, the populations of these organisms in the soil should die away between crops. And third, as the soil for different crops is prepared and cultivated in different ways, a rotation scheme should ensure that shallow cultivations and possible problems from the development of a hard, water-trapping pan in the soil aren't restricted permanently to one area.

There are in practice, however, serious shortcomings. The nutrient argument seems reasonable enough but how many gardeners really do know the difference between a crop with a high requirement for potash and one with a high requirement for phosphate? And how many gardeners of your acquaintance actually rely on the amount of nutrient present in the soil? Not many. Ninety per cent of gardeners give a handful or two (or three) of a balanced general fertiliser such as Growmore or fish, blood and bone and are well satisfied with the results. So any shortcomings in the soil are soon overcome.

And I think the idea that there are benefits in controlling pest and disease to be had from crop rotation in a garden is specious. The theory is sound enough but it depends on two principles: first, that many pests, fungi and bacteria are fairly specific to individual types of host plant and can't survive on other types of plant and second, that the period over which such organisms can survive in the soil in the absence of the correct plant is very limited. There are exceptions to the first category: the familiar grey mould fungus (Botrytis) and the potato-peach aphid, for instance, both affect a very wide range of plants. There are some organisms that can survive for very many years in the soil; the clubroot-causing fungus and the onion white rot fungus, which can last in the soil for over 20 years, are just two of them.

Unfortunately, however, much of this aspect of crop rotation theory was established in commercial horticulture and farming where the distances between the site in which a crop is grown in one year and that to which it is moved the next may be considerable. In a garden or allotment the distance is likely to be a few metres at the most, and the conventional three-course garden crop rotation takes no account of the fact that many pests can fly or even that soil contaminated with clubroot or other organisms will be moved on spades, wheelbarrows and gardeners' boots. With few exceptions therefore, such as minimising the likelihood of eelworm becoming established in potatoes, I don't think the benefits in controlling pest and disease are very real.

So we come to the third use of rotation: that of helping to ensure that the whole vegetable garden is cultivated uniformly. Here I do believe there are genuine merits, whether you use the deep bed system of cropping or the more traditional row cropping technique. Just think of the difference in soil disturbance and cultivation between growing a crop of potatoes on the one hand and onions on the other and I think you will see what I mean.

So rotate by all means; it will give some benefits and if nothing else it will help vary the view from your kitchen window. And try as far as possible to follow the usual three-course system that I mentioned earlier. Divide your vegetable garden into three plots of more or less equal area. And think of your crops in

RIGHT: *The increased popularity in recent years of leaf lettuces such as the Italian 'Lollo Rosso' and 'Lollo Biondo' has meant that the kitchen garden has become both productive and attractive.*

I'm bewildered by the range of lettuces in my seed catalogue. Can you help?

I don't think that any kitchen garden vegetable has seen such a multiplicity of new varieties in recent years as lettuce. Largely this has arisen because of the increased appreciation of leafy or non-hearting varieties for cut-and-come again salads. They make much better use of the ground area, which is especially valuable in a small garden.

There are still three main groups of hearting lettuce: the rather soft-leaved, rounded varieties called cabbage, smooth or butterhead lettuce; the curly-leaved crisphead types (often called 'Webbs' after the best known, 'Webbs Wonderful') and the upright, rather cylindrical cos lettuces. Nonetheless, there are varieties between categories that are intermediate in appearance. One recent change has come from the introduction of several miniature variants which are far more useful for the average family and result in less wastage. The little butterhead variety 'Tom Thumb' and the miniature cos 'Little Gem' have been the most important and, I think, the best of these.

It was the introduction of the curly-leaved Italian leaf varieties 'Lollo Rosso' and 'Lollo Biondo' some years ago that presaged a big

change. Along with 'Salad Bowl', they offered masses of leaf but no heart, something that previously was achieved only by accident or by close spacing of normal hearting lettuce. Much of the development in these varieties since has been in colour, for in addition to the red-leaved (more accurately, dark purple) 'Lollo Rosso', there are now 'Red Salad Bowl', 'Red Sails', 'Sigma', 'Valeria' and others, with greater or lesser leaf coloration and degree of frill.

My own favourites, both for appearance and flavour, are the oak-leaved varieties. To be honest, the leaves tend to look more like dandelion than oak leaves, but with their pure green and reddish colorations they are extremely pretty. Some are pure leaf lettuces but some will heart given time.

Don't forget, however, that there are also varying degrees of hardiness among lettuce varieties and it's important to choose winter-hardy types for cold greenhouse or cloche production out of season.

terms of three main groups: root crops, the pea and bean family, and brassicas and similar leafy vegetables. Then use the following cropping sequence:

	PLOT A	PLOT B	PLOT C
year 1	Roots	Peas and beans	Leafy crops
year 2	Peas and beans	Leafy crops	Roots
year 3	Leafy crops	Roots	Peas and beans

There will be exceptions and, of course, if you don't happen to like one particular crop you will have space to spare. And there will be some crops such as runner beans that can be grown in the same area for many years, unless and until their yield begins to drop away seriously. And finally, you will have a few quick-growing plants such as lettuce and radishes that can be slotted in among other things as space allows. Don't be a slave to rotation but try to use it as the basis for your vegetable gardening.

There will also be a small number of perennial vegetables such as rhubarb and asparagus that will have their own, more or less permanent beds, outside the main rotation plots. If disease doesn't arise in them, they need never be moved.

New and improved hybrid plants and their virtues

GARDENING IS A CONSTANTLY evolving activity and many aspects of the subject today would be quite alien to our fathers and grandfathers. I don't think that there is any way in which matters have changed so greatly however as in the increase of hybrids in gardens. Only in the garden of the serious plantsman today are you likely to see more than a small number of unaltered species. Gardening is now about the growing of hybrids and, in some areas, about the growing of what are called F_1 hybrids. Why?

A hybrid is the offspring of two genetically different individuals. They may be varieties that have arisen in cultivation (cultivars), natural varieties, subspecies, species or, very occasionally genera. Often they are sterile and so unable to reproduce sexually. They must therefore be propagated by other means: by divisions, cuttings or grafts for example. But why go to the trouble? What is it about hybrids that makes them so important? It is partly because hybridisation offers a means of combining the features of two separate plants in one individual. For example, perhaps there are two fairly similar and closely related species, one having large red flowers and the other smaller yellow ones. If they are crossed artificially, the seed collected and the offspring grown, there will be a mixture of plants with flowers of varying size and colour. It's then possible to select those individuals that have the biggest and most yellow flowers. If, in turn, seed is collected from them, you can gradually develop a population of plants that consistently have flowers both big and yellow. Hence one virtue of a hybrid.

But there's another important virtue. Hybridisation was once referred to as 'improving', and the use of this term reveals much about the nature of gardeners. We are never satisfied with what nature has supplied but always trying to change it to meet our own criteria of excellence. Generally, a hybrid, whether it's a plant or a mongrel dog, tends to be larger and in some way more vigorous than its parents. But if a hybrid plant is allowed to perpetuate itself by further cross-pollination, it will still be fairly variable. It is known as an open-pollinated hybrid. In recent years, however, even this variability has been found to be a disadvantage, especially by commercial growers who, for reasons of marketing and ease of harvesting, prefer their crops not only large but also uniformly large and maturing at the same time. These requirements have led to the development of F_1 hybrid cultivars, and this is a classification that you will see increasingly in seed catalogues.

An F_1 hybrid is produced by repeatedly inbreeding two groups of plant; that is, keeping them separate and crossing them for generation after generation. Once two 'pure' groups have been produced, each with some particularly desirable feature, they are crossed together to combine these features.

Despite what your seed catalogues might imply however, the F_1 hybrid is not necessarily always better than the open-pollinated one and there are several features of F_1 hybrids that are worth considering before you buy them. The uniformity so beloved of the commercial grower who wishes to harvest an entire field of cabbages with one pass of his automated cutting machine may not be so desirable for gardeners. We usually prefer cabbages to mature more irregularly over several weeks for use in the kitchen. And the giant flower heads of bedding plants such as some of the F_1 hybrid African and French marigolds are not to everyone's liking, wonderful as they may appear and appropriate as they may be on a municipal traffic island. Size and uniformity should be considered carefully, therefore, before you place all of your eggs in the basket of the F_1 hybrid.

Almost invariably, F_1 hybrid seed is more expensive than that of open-pollinated plants because its production is costly and labour-intensive. The inbred groups of plants must be maintained carefully away from any possible contaminating pollen. And the actual crosses between them must usually be performed very carefully by trained hands to avoid the transfer of pollen onto a stigma of the same plant. Even then, tricks may be needed. Tricks such as bud-pollination, where the pollen is transferred to the stigma of an unopened flower before its own pollen-bearing stamens have matured. Or pollination of flowers from which the stamens have been removed artificially.

An alternative to hand-pollination is to use insects and breed the feature of self-incompatibility into the inbred plants, although this itself is a lengthy and expensive process. Plants that naturally are self-pollinating, such as lettuces and French beans, are difficult to develop as F_1 hybrids, and with results that generally don't repay the effort involved. In other instances, there may already be acceptable uniformity in the open-pollinated varieties.

But before I leave the subject of F_1 hybrids, it's worth making two more points. There's great fun and satisfaction to be had from saving seed from your own garden plants. But

How can I ensure a good set of pods on my runner beans?

This must be the commonest question and the biggest frustration in runner bean growing. The short answer is that there is no way to guarantee a good set, especially of the first few trusses low down on the plants, but you can do a few things to help matters. Lack of moisture close to soil level is often the reason for failure to set, and hot dry weather in early summer can mean a poor crop. You should therefore ensure that the plants are well-watered and also well-mulched as soon as they begin to climb.

The objective is to obtain satisfactory pollination and it's useful to realise that, moisture or not, runner beans aren't all pollinated with equal facility. Although all varieties are self-fertile, the visit of a bee or other insect is necessary to bring pollen into contact with the stigma. This seems to

happen much more readily with the white-flowered types, like my favourite 'White Emergo', than with the more familiar red-flowered varieties, so you may find that the white-flowered forms succeed better where pod set is a problem.

It's also worth remembering that birds, and especially sparrows, may remove the young flower buds, and this will also help reduce the number of pods. If birds are a persistent problem, then netting the plants might prove beneficial, although it must be realised that this can also exclude pollinating insects. As I have implied, there just isn't an easy answer.

saving seed from an F_1 hybrid is a waste of time for it will almost certainly result in a total hotchpotch of very variable plants, as a result of cross-pollination within the population and with other varieties growing nearby. And if the very high degree of uniformity and very high cost of F_1 hybrids doesn't appeal to you, the greater variability and lower cost of F_2 hybrids might. This is especially so with such plants as pelargoniums, for which seed of open-pollinated varieties is unavailable. An F_2 hybrid is produced by carefully allowing a population of F_1 hybrid plants to pollinate together freely, but still preventing any cross-pollination with other cultivars. It's more variable than an F_1 but still acceptably uniform.

Have vegetables really lost their flavour?

I'VE MENTIONED ELSEWHERE in the book the rather widely held belief that in the garden, 'things aren't what they used to be'. 'Things' used to be better, and I'm told that in no area were they once better than in the taste of the plants we grow. I remember once upsetting the Potato Marketing Board on this subject. I was asked a question on a radio programme about slug control. The questioner didn't want to use slug pellets because he thought it might be possible to taste them when he ate the crop. I asked him which variety he grew, to which the answer was 'Maris Piper'. My response was that anyone growing 'Maris Piper' should appreciate any flavour, even of slug pellets. The Potato Marketing Board Chairman wrote to me the same week to defend his biggest-selling variety.

And therein lies part of the explanation. 'Maris Piper' is such an important commercial variety because it is high-yielding, relatively easy to grow, and relatively resistant to pest and disease problems; all important features. But its flavour comes rather far down the list. And so it is with many varieties of fruit and vegetables. Crops are grown commercially and the economics of commercial growing demand such features, together with thick skins for long shelf-life, uniform maturity, size and shape for ease of packing and transport. If you buy your fruit and vegetables from a shop, then these are the features that you will encounter.

In a garden, you have a much wider choice. Varieties, old varieties in many instances, that no longer are considered commercially viable are still available. And if it is the best flavour you want, then it is some of these you should grow. I don't claim that all old varieties taste good but conversely, I can think of few instances in kitchen garden crops where a modern variety

My Brussels sprouts are loose and badly formed. Why is this?

We have grown so accustomed to the type of Brussels sprout that supermarkets offer to us, that it's easy to forget that they have ever been any different. The modern shop sprout is hard, round and dark green. They originate on F_1 hybrid varieties that crop uniformly and are grown under carefully controlled conditions. If you grow older, open-pollinated or non-F_1 types therefore, you must expect some variation in texture. But loose or 'blown' sprouts can arise for other reasons.

tastes appreciably better than anything that went before. I suppose that tomatoes such as 'Gardeners' Delight' and 'Sungold' are among the more notable exceptions. But even they aren't considered good commercial types.

So by growing your own, chosen varieties, flavour can return to your dining table. And by eating them freshly picked or harvested, even more flavour will return. For there's no doubt that the fresher the produce when it's eaten, the better the flavour. Despite the technology of what is known as the 'cold chain', the use of refrigerated transport from field through warehouse to shop, unavoidable chemical changes in the harvested crop, once it ceases to grow, inevitably mean an alteration in taste.

Another argument often heard is that modern crops have worse flavour because of the use of artificial fertiliser. And here, I find the arguments are harder to sustain. Vegetables taste better I'm told, if they are grown with organic fertilisers. But bear in mind that plants are unable to distinguish between artificials and organics. They don't absorb ammonium sulphate or dried blood; they absorb nitrogen, and nitrogen is the same no matter where it originated. And so it is with other essential nutrients too. Plants absorb them in simple forms that are always the same, irrespective of the fertiliser in which they were applied. Taste moreover is a very subjective business. If you think you can detect a difference that can be attributed solely to the type of fertiliser used, all well and good. It might have some scientific basis but there's no evidence for it. And in view of the enormous range of chemical processes that go to make up the phenomenon that we call flavour, I'm always amazed, not so much that the type of fertiliser can affect it, but that an organic fertiliser always changes it in ways that we find an improvement. Use organic fertilisers or artificial ones; but don't make flavour part of the equation.

Although all brassicas require a good deal of nitrogen, over-dosing can sometimes cause looseness. Water is important too, but over-watering may also add to the problem. Water the plants thoroughly at transplanting and if you are growing them closely spaced (as you might in a small garden), water throughout the life of the crop. If they are at the more conventional spacing of around 45cm, they should need additional water after transplanting only in very dry years and in times of drought.

But perhaps the commonest reason for loose sprouts is that the plants are not planted firmly enough. On a windy and exposed site, especially with a light soil, they should also be staked. Incorporate plenty of organic matter on a light soil and grow the shorter-stemmed types such as 'Peer Gynt' which are less prone to being top-heavy.

AGAINST THE ELEMENTS

Scotland is a land of gardening contrasts. There are mild and sheltered spots in the lowlands as gentle as any in England, but its magnificent wild Highlands are the spiritual home of mountain plants and rock gardening, and present some of the greatest horticultural challenges of nature.

The effect of wind on plant growth

PREVIOUS PAGE:
*This herbaceous
border at Crathes
Castle shows the
beautiful results that
can be achieved, even
in the northernmost
reaches of Britain.*

PRETTY WELL ALL gardeners understand and appreciate the impact on their gardens of warm weather in summer, frosts in winter and spring and of plenty of water. By and large, unless they live in high or otherwise very exposed areas, they tend to forget about one of the most important of all environmental features, the wind. It becomes evident if a fence is blown down or a tree uprooted in a gale, but its day-by-day significance is, overall, much greater.

Apart from the dramatic one-off results of gales, wind affects our gardens, and plants in general, in two quite distinct ways. On the one hand it is essential to their long-term survival, while on the other, it can work to their short-term detriment. On the first theme, wind, after insects, is the most important medium for the transfer of pollen from one flower to another for fertilisation to occur and seeds and fruit to form. In exposed gardens, however, where the prevailing wind is very strong, the effect may be to blow away the pollen so quickly that it is unable to do its task. Some shelter may be needed therefore to obtain proper fruit set in such exposed places.

But once seeds and fruits have been produced, the effect of wind becomes important again. For it is by wind movement that many are carried away from the parent plant to enable new plants to grow and new parts of the soil to be colonised.

In the wild, this wind dispersal is important for the spread of plant species. In gardens, it isn't our cultivated plants that are affected by this as much as their natural competitors, the weeds. Wind can play a very significant part in the spread of weeds, and its action underlines

What are the most effective types of garden windbreak?

The same wind that is important to plants for pollination and for seed dispersal can adversely affect plant growth. And so it is evident that a windbreak can only improve matters. Indeed, in exposed gardens, it may be the complete key to growing plants successfully. When choosing a windbreak, you must bear in mind two important considerations. First, that the optimum effect is achieved if the windbreak is 50% permeable; in other words, if it has as much gap as solid material. The reason is that a completely solid barrier causes powerful eddies which may themselves be damaging and causes material blown by the

the importance in weed control of removing them before they have had the chance to become established and flower.

But against the beneficial effects to plants of pollen and seed movement must be set the fact that it's also on the wind that most fungal spores and many garden pests are carried. Although this has relatively little importance within an individual garden, it can be highly significant for the larger scale spread of plant problems. Moreover, coastal winds, laden with salt, can have a major damaging effect on those types of garden plants that are not adapted to coastal conditions (see pages 25-29) and this underlines the importance of choosing plants appropriate to your garden's position. And there is a modern industrial equivalent to salt damage, for plants can be adversely affected by chemicals blown from factories situated many kilometres away upwind.

Nonetheless, it's the drying effect of the wind that I think is of the greatest (and least appreciated) importance for plants. But here again, it is a matter of degree. It's because the wind evaporates water from leaf surfaces that more water can be drawn up from the soil below and the plant is maintained in a viable condition. But enough wind can soon become too much. The rate of drying at the leaf surface can easily exceed the rate at which the roots are able to take up moisture. This can affect plant growth in several ways. Very strong, drying winds cause buds to shrivel and so the growth of the plant on the side facing the wind is adversely affected. The result is trees and shrubs like those seen at the seaside, which seem permanently to be leaning away from the sea. They haven't been blown down, but they have been pruned by the wind.

wind to collect on the leeward side. A permeable barrier, in allowing some of the wind to pass through, avoids this problem. And second, the benefits from a windbreak operate for a distance downwind of approximately twenty times its height. A barrier 2m high will therefore lessen the force of the wind for about 40m.

But of course, the windbreak must itself be robust. The best windbreaks are living ones; trees for large areas and hedges for normal sized gardens. But of course, a hedge takes time to grow and so an attractive option is to plant a hedge but put a fence alongside it to provide shelter while the hedge matures. The fence must of course be strong and well-supported: stakes penetrating the ground to a depth of about 1m and braced. And for a strong, but 50% permeable fence, you will find that willow hurdles work well in all except the very windiest places. The familiar panels of overlapping softwood planks will be destroyed very quickly in exposed gardens.

During drought periods in the summer, the amount of water in the soil is simply inadequate to replace that lost through the leaves and in consequence, plants wilt. But in winter too, evergreen plants continue to lose water by evaporation and whilst the soil may be full of moisture, plants simply can't use it if the ground is frozen. The idea of a drought in the middle of winter must seem odd, but the results are equally devastating.

Up to a point, plants can tolerate water shortages and will recover when water becomes available again. But beyond that point, irreparable damage to the cells is caused and part, or all of the plant, will die. Even if they survive, however, constant exposure to wind will stunt growth overall and if you compare plants of the same species growing in a wild, exposed garden and those in one lying in a sheltered valley bottom, the difference may be so great that they are barely recognisable as the same. All of this underlines the importance of shelter in a garden (see box, pages 88-89).

The secret of obtaining a balance in a water garden

FOR MANY GARDENERS, water gardens and rock gardens are natural companions, just as tarns and lakes are natural accompaniments of mountains. I'm certain that water gardening has never been more popular. In

ABOVE: *Shrubs growing in exposed windy areas commonly have some of their buds dried off in a process called wind pruning which results in a curiously flattened shape.*

RIGHT: *The richness of plants available for waterside planting can match, if not surpass, that of any herbaceous border.*

large part, surely this is due to the wide range of excellent pond materials and equipment now available. You can decide today to have a pond and almost, by tomorrow, it will be in place. And also in its favour is the fact that a pond can be relevant and appropriate to almost any type of garden. The hard edges and straight lines of the formal pond are right for a formal garden just as the soft banks and graded planting of a semi-natural one are for the informal garden.

Pond gardening isn't without its difficulties and every year I meet people who have problems, as they say, in 'getting the balance right'. In some measure, I think the reason is that gardeners do what, under normal circumstances, I warmly recommend: they have looked at the way that nature does it. This means going further than the town park with its boating pool or even the village duck pond, for all such things are man-made. It means going out into the hills and mountains to see tarns and lakes. They are filled by water draining along a stream course or even percolating directly through the soil itself. They remain at a more or less constant level but will overflow, after heavy rainfall, into the surrounding land. They contain fish of varying species, sizes and ages that breed and produce young, numerous other water animals and various kinds of aquatic vegetation. And they are generally fringed with shrubs or even fairly large trees that overhang the water.

Now try and reproduce this in your own garden and you will very soon be in serious trouble. The water level won't stay constant through the medium of rainfall. It will drop dramatically in summer and it will overflow,

I have a stream running through my garden; can you suggest plants for the streamside?

The gardeners I envy most are those who have a stream of their own. In saying this, I should perhaps offer one or two cautionary words. Although the stream may flow through your garden, you will almost certainly not be its sole owner. You will own the bed and the banks but probably not the water. You will probably have no rights to remove the water without permission, possibly no rights to fish and almost certainly none to obstruct the flow. The latter in particular should be borne in mind when planting the banks.

It's important to realise that a stream bank isn't exactly the same as either a bog garden or the marginal area of a pond. The water in a stream rises and falls and the banks, even very close to the water surface, may become very dry in summer but then be totally inundated in winter.

equally dramatically, in winter. Fish there may be, but they will usually be of the golden kind and whilst they may breed, you will be very fortunate if they maintain, over the years, a self-sustaining population. Water plants will probably be there too but again, unless you are fortunate, at least one species will embark upon rampant growth to the extent that it chokes everything else. And it will be followed by plant growth of a rather more primitive kind in the shape of green algae, both unicellular and filamentous (blanket weed) which will envelop all else. And those trees that so picturesquely overhang the water's edge? They will shed leaves into the water at a rate faster than you can remove them. The leaves will sink, rot, release noxious gases and the end result will be a foul-smelling soup of neither use nor ornament.

So why are really natural ponds so successful and our attempts at copying them so disastrous? It's due, very largely, to the scale of the thing. The volume of leaves in relation to the volume of water in a natural pond is greatly different from that in our garden. There is room moreover for fish of different kinds to live, hide and work out their lives without colliding with each other. The balance of gases is such that the water doesn't become foul and there are usually ducks and other large creatures on hand to keep weed growth in check.

In a garden, the secret in creating what I much prefer to call an informal rather than a natural pond, is in making it look like a real one but without the difficulties. When you make the pool, be sure to have 'soft' edges so that the water almost laps against the banks. Make sure also that your pool liner extends well above the

Nonetheless, given these considerations, the world is your oyster and the plants that follow are merely a taster of what is possible. Personally, I have to say that I prefer to see either a planting of native plants on streamside or a planting of exotics; but not a conflicting mixture.

NATIVE PLANTS
Acorus calamus (Sweet flag)
Butomus umbellatus (Flowering rush)
Filipendula ulmaria (Meadow sweet)
Geum rivale (Water Avens)
Iris pseudacorus (Flag iris)
Lythrum salicaria (Purple loosestrife)
Myrica gale (Bog myrtle)
Osmunda regalis (Royal fern)
Trollius europaeus (Globe flower)

EXOTIC PLANTS

Astilbe species
Dodecatheon 'Shooting Stars'
Gunnera mannicata
Hosta sieboldiana (Plantain lily)
Iris species (Water iris)
Phyllostachys nigra (Black bamboo)
Primula florindae (Himalayan cowslip)
Rodgersia pinnata
Zantedeschia aethiopica (Arum lily)

water surface and beneath the surrounding rocks and vegetation to prevent the pond overflowing. Make the pool as large as you can given the available space. Give fish plenty of places to hide and be sure that the only large shrubs that you plant close by are evergreen.

Then, be prepared to manage it; to top up the water as necessary, to remove blanket weed and excessive plant growth (and do be sure to plant the less invasive species of aquatic plant, such as small water lilies and golden club). Give your fish artificial food to supplement what is available naturally, try to keep the water well-aerated by means of a small circulating fountain or similar device, and above all, do be sure to remove, manually, any leaves that blow in from elsewhere in the neighbourhood. I can't promise you that the water won't be pea green or that there will be no blanket weed. In fact, pea green water is caused by a 'bloom' of microscopic green algae which proliferate at certain times of the year and die away at others. Blanket weed really must be pulled out by hand; don't use chemical controls. They will result in dead blanket weed that will in turn rot and foul the water.

Great Highland gardens

IF BRITAIN AS a whole is a land of great gardening contrasts, those contrasts are magnified in Scotland. The distance from the west to east coasts is in places no more than a handful of kilometres but the climatic difference is great. The western influence of the Gulf Steam and the eastern exposure to the North Sea create markedly different environments. As you journey north and the land mass widens, the contrast becomes greater still and the great gardens of Aberdeenshire, Moray and Nairn, Kincardine and Deeside, Angus and the west of Perth and Kinross could be worlds apart from the western havens like Inverewe in Ross and Cromarty or Crarae in Argyll. In their magnificent formality, these eastern gardens owe more to man than to nature and find their closest counterparts in some of the great old gardens of England.

Crathes Castle near Banchory is a twentieth-century garden although its structure defies you to believe this. The house really is a castle and dates from the late sixteenth century. The oldest plantings are those that today give

LEFT: *This magnificent doocot (dovecote) at Crathes Castle dates from the early nineteenth century although the garden surrounding it is, remarkably, a modern one.*

95

the garden its enduring character: the great yew hedges were planted in 1702 and serve to subdivide the garden. It always strikes me, the more gardens I see, that the secret of success linking so many of them is the very fact that they aren't single entities but have been divided into smaller parts, each more manageable to be sure, but each also endowed with a different character. It is a feature that has become a hallmark of twentieth-century British gardening.

The hedges at Crathes puff and billow like inflated old gentlemen, neatly shaved at the edges to give their sculptured form an added fascination. Together with smoothly shaped Portugal laurels and fine stone walls they presented the ideal environment in which Sir James and Lady Burnett, whose ancestors had been granted the land at Crathes in 1323, planted their series of individual, beautifully formed gardens between the wars. The Croquet Lawn closest to the house, the Pool garden with its three themed colours of yellow, red and purple, the Fountain Garden with its central Florentine statue and the Rose Garden, holding old and modern varieties in combination with lavender, comprise the four gardens closest to the house. They rightly reflect the formality both of the building and the ancient boundaries. Further away, the White Border, with its white, silvers and greys, contrasts with the riotous herbaceous fury of the June border. But it's only by subdividing the site that such things can happily coexist within a few metres walking distance.

Topiary exists at Crathes, just as it does and I think should, in any formal garden. But for some of the most under-appreciated and wonderful topiary in any British garden, you must

Can you recommend a list of shrubs that will tolerate exposure to the cold?

Many shrubs are cold-tolerant but relatively few are evergreens. Any plant bearing foliage at a time of the year when frost and, more importantly, very cold winds prevail, is always likely to suffer from browning. I have included all of those evergreens that in my experience have been reasonably tolerant of at least moderately cold winters. In extreme conditions, all may suffer browning but will recover by summer.

Arctostaphylos uva-ursi (Bearberry). A creeping alpine with pink white flowers and red berries. Acid soils. Evergreen.

Calluna vulgaris (Heather). Many varieties with flowers in white, pink or red. Acid soils. Evergreen.

travel south, to the west of Perthshire and the ancestral lands of the Drummonds. Close to Errol, you will find one of the Drummond homes in the fifteenth-century, turreted Megginch Castle. The gardens at Megginch boast some fine herbaceous borders but it's the topiary that unavoidably takes your eye. Planted in the late nineteenth century, you will find all of the

Cornus alba (Red barked dogwood). Varieties with variously coloured leaves and stems. Prune hard for winter stem colour.

Cornus stolonifera. Vigorous suckering plant with red stems. Good for wilder exposed places.

Cotinus coggygria (Smoke bush). Best flower effect is in full sun.

Euonymus fortunei. Trailing, ground cover shrub with many varieties, differing in vigour and leaf patterning. Evergreen.

Gaultheria mucronata. Dwarf, forming dense thickets with white, heather-like flowers and round fruits, varying with variety from white to purple. Acid soils. Evergreen.

Gaultheria shallon (Partridge berry). Vigorous thicket-forming shrub. Acid soil. Evergreen.

Hippophae rhamnoides (Sea buckthorn). Narrow, silver leaves and orange-yellow berries on female plants.

Kalmia angustifolia. Beautiful rich flowers in spring. Acid soils. Evergreen.

Kerria japonica (Jew's mallow). Upright habit, cane-like stems. Orange spring flowers.

Leucothoe fontanesiana. Graceful arching stems with white pendant flowers. Acid soils. Evergreen.

Lonicera pileata. Dwarf with tiny, bright green leaves. Evergreen.

Mahonia aquifolium (Oregon grape). Holly-like glossy leaves and scented bright yellow spring flowers. Evergreen.

Philadelphus coronarius (Mock orange). Many varieties of varying size and vigour. Scented white flowers in early summer.

Pieris floribunda. More or less dwarf, mound-forming shrub with masses of tiny white flowers. Acid soils. Evergreen.

Rhododendron species. Wide range of varieties, 'Hardy Hybrids' and flower colour. Acid soils. Evergreen.

Salix species (Willows). Huge range of varieties and species. Choose less vigorous types for close to buildings.

Spiraea species. Huge range of varieties but among the prettiest are the white-flowered forms of *Spiraea* x *arguta.*

Ulex (Gorse). Vivid golden flowers in spring on a dense, very thorny low-growing shrub. Excellent as a barrier plant.

Viburnum opulus (Guelder rose). Large, robust shrub with leaves like an Acer; the best autumn colour shrub for cold places.

expected and familiar figures of topiary: animals, birds and geometric shapes. But in a very real sense, the crowning achievement is the planting that celebrated both Queen Victoria's Diamond Jubilee in 1887 and the golden wedding of Frances and John Drummond in 1885. A fantastic hollow crown of gold and green yew is fashioned over a gigantic iron framework that just invites you to walk beneath. And ponder the foresight of the planting that must have been a full 50 years old before it really began to take on its intended form. But such is the gardener's role; part practical and functional, part sheer optimistic visionary.

Pitmedden is different from them both, and probably different from anything you will see anywhere. It lies to the north of Aberdeen and is a property of the National Trust for Scotland. The seventeenth-century house has gone, destroyed by fire, but it is a garden to be visited to obtain a glimpse into the past. For Pitmedden is a recreated garden, a recreation of a garden that existed here in the late seventeenth century when Sir Alexander Seton, first baronet of Pitmedden, laid out his 'Great Garden'. In a huge walled site, the stone walls buttressed by yew, are some 5km of dwarf box hedging that outline four great formal parterres in geometric patterns. Three of the parterres are plantings based on designs that may once have been used at Holyrood, the fourth displays the Seton family crest. Fantastic they are, although best seen, as Sir William never managed, from a helicopter. But it is a pity that the plantings today are in modern bedding plants to give the brightness that is supposedly now expected. The original herbs must have been softer indeed. Perhaps that is being too conservative. For these three Scottish gardens in their different ways do display that no garden is some static creation, frozen at a chosen moment in time. They are living, dynamic, changing; and if Sir William Seton had had fibrous-rooted begonias in his armoury, who are we to say that he wouldn't have planted them with vigour.

The history of the rock garden

I'M NOT SURE why rock gardening came so late onto the horticultural scene. Surely, people in times past must have noticed the beauty of the plants of the mountains, if only of the more accessible high mountain

valleys. Perhaps it was simply that alpine plants had few obvious medicinal or culinary attributes, which was for centuries, of course, the serious reason for growing plants in gardens. It was, I think, mountaineering, or what passed for mountaineering in the nineteenth century, that was the real impetus for men and women wanting to carry home and grow some of the quite glorious flowers that they found.

Yet therein lies one of the great difficulties, great challenges and yet great blessings of alpine or rock gardening. There is such a wide diversity of plant types, representatives of so many families that no one set of conditions satisfies all. That wasn't immediately obvious however to our forefathers and the oldest rock garden is probably that at the Chelsea Physic garden in London, built in 1772 with a collection of old rocks from the Tower of London, lava from Iceland and some bits of chalk and flint. For many years, such irregular piles of rocks, sometimes with old tree trunks thrown in for good measure, were what passed for rock gardens. Stoneries they were called, or to sound more classical, lapideums. Things improved slightly in the early years of the nineteenth century when it was thought that a miniature scale reproduction of the Alps was called for. Both large and small gardens sprouted forth little mountain ranges, sometimes with artificial snow to cap the peaks. Where the scale was such that the tiny plants were some metres distant from the nearest path, garden visitors were supplied with telescopes to view the flora. Miniature Swiss chalets completed the picture.

Gradually, however, a degree of naturalism and rather more meaningful scale appeared and some of the best of the early rock gardens, as now, were in those gardens where a natural stone outcrop could be capitalised upon.

My rock garden is pretty in spring but then looks rather dull; have you any advice?

It's a popular misconception that rock gardens are only for the spring. Certainly, there are proportionately more rock plants with spring flowers but there is evidence in my own garden to prove that a rock garden needn't be dull for any part of the year. I've therefore selected a number of plants and plant types that don't have spring as their main time of interest and that are worth considering as you plan your all-season rock garden:

Arabis alpina caucasica	Early spring
Armeria maritima	Early summer
Aster alpinus	Early–midsummer
Dodecatheon species	Early–midsummer
Gentiana sino-ornata	Autumn
Geranium cinereum	Early–midsummer
Hepatica nobilis	Winter–early spring
Leontopodium alpinum	Early summer
Lithospermum diffusum	Summer
Polygonum vaccinifolium	Autumn–winter
Potentilla nitida	Summer
Primula vialii	Early summer
Ranunculus gramineus	Early summer
Sempervivum species	Summer
Silene maritima	Late summer
Sisyrinchium species	Late summer–autumn
Veronica prostrata	Early summer

Even where there was no natural rock, the importance of adhering to the type that occurred naturally in the area was paramount, and arranging the rock in a semblance of bedding planes was more widely attempted. Gradually too, the goal shifted from trying to recreate a rock garden to creating a rock plant garden, the emphasis being on finding the correct way to cultivate the alpine flora. No-one more exemplified this approach than the forthright Reginald Farrer. He was a remarkable character who, with some justification, has been called the Father of Rock Gardening. Born in Yorkshire in 1880 and educated at Balliol, he became fascinated with the mountain flora and combed the Alps for plants in the early years of the present century, telling of his exploits in a series of rather extraordinary books. Farrer's florid writing takes some adjusting to, but although sometimes imitated, it has never been matched. He was utterly dismissive of the 'mountain-range' rock gardens of the time and set out his views most comprehensively in an encyclopaedic work that is still unmatched, *The English Rock Garden*. Just before and shortly after the First World War, Farrer visited China and Tibet and then, extensively, Burma, collecting and bringing back many worthy plants. Not all by any means were alpines and personally I shall thank him every June for *Buddleja alternifolia*.

In gardens, and thanks to Farrer's influence, the stones became smaller and fewer, the beds themselves smaller and often raised. The so-called table or billiard table bed became popular and has remained so. This had the advantages of bringing the plants, most of which are small, closer to eye-level, the better to see their beauty. And the elevated bed, built up with soil and rocks, facilitated the free-draining conditions that these plants of alpine origin require.

On a very small scale, alpines can be grown in troughs (see box below). The importance of conserving our natural rock landscape has led to a move against the use of rocks in the home garden, unless they be of artificial, replica stone. To see good outdoor rock gardens today, built may it be said with carefully sourced stone, you will do no better than visit some of the great public gardens. The Royal Botanic Garden at Edinburgh has appropriately always had a large and fine rock garden while that at Wisley, extensively rebuilt in recent years, can now match the best. And on another plane, the rock gardens that have graced the Chelsea Flower Show for many years continue to delight and entrance visitors, amazed both at the naturalism and that such enduring-looking gardens can be created within three weeks.

BELOW: *The days when rock gardens meant a recreation of the Alps have long gone. Wonderful small gardens can be created in alpine troughs.*

How can I grow rock garden plants in limited space?

Few people these days have room for a rock garden in the traditional style. And it is so difficult to build a rock garden that looks remotely natural that I'm not at all sure that some alternative should not be the norm. In moderately sized gardens, a series of hollow wall-beds, with compost and plants between two containing walls, can be very appealing. But there's no doubt that most attractive of all, and adaptable to gardens of any size, are containers.

Containers for alpines really mean stone troughs. Nothing else looks as good or effective. But of course real stone troughs are now prohibitively expensive. There are fortunately some very good artificial stone replicas and it's perfectly possible, by using hypertufa, to create excellent ones yourself, using an old sink as the base, which can then be covered with the hypertufa. All you need do is ensure that there is adequate drainage and that you are using a very free-draining, gritty soil-based compost and you can plant away to your heart's content. I would advise only that you check on the vigour of your chosen plants. Choose the cushion-forming rather than mat-forming types that won't swamp their companions.

The bonny banks of heather

ABOVE: *The relatively
few species of wild
heather have given
rise, in cultivation,
to an astonishing
array of types with
different flower and
foliage colours.*

ON SOME TOPICS, gardeners constantly argue. But on others, you will
find almost total agreement. And if you ask a sample of gardeners to name
the one plant that sums up Scotland, or even sums up mountainous areas in
general, the answer will be the heather. And in saying this, everyone will
immediately conjure up an image of craggy hillsides in summer, the ground
covered with a mauve carpet, almost too ethereal to touch.

In truth this is only a small part of the picture. The plant they are imagin-
ing and the plant that every home-sick Scotsman sees in his mind's eye is
Calluna vulgaris, the so-called common heather, also known as ling, its old
Norse name. It's a native British plant and also occurs extensively throughout much of Europe as far east as the Urals. Like so many plants of acidic
soils, it belongs, along with around 100 other genera, including *Arbutus,
Gaultheria, Kalmia, Pieris*, and *Rhododendron* to the family *Ericaceae*.
Nonetheless, in such a huge family, *Calluna* is unusual in that there is only
one species. This it makes up for in being pretty variable, and no doubt

Scottish crofters in centuries past spotted plants with differently coloured flowers, especially the striking white ones, and planted them close to their homes. So the cultivation of the heather began, but its propensity for variation is such that since horticulturists have had their hands on it, well over 1000 varieties in cultivation have resulted.

The variation now available in *Calluna* isn't only in flower colour, although a huge range of reds, pinks and purples does exist, but also in foliage colour (and foliage colour changes in winter) and size. It's size indeed where the greatest variation of all is to be found, from prostrate plants like 'Hibernica' and the minute, cushion-forming 'Foxii Nana' at one end of the spectrum to varieties such as 'Robert Chapman' which are some 70cm in height and spread. Even so, variable as the wild species is, looking at the countless thousands of plants carpeting the Scottish mountains, one does sometimes wonder just where all of these extremes originated.

Calluna heathers aren't difficult to grow provided you remember their essential needs. They must, positively must, have an acidic soil; they require plenty of moisture (preferably a high rainfall); and a soil that is not too rich, but is well-draining. This is all very well but there are many gardeners who love heathers and yet can offer neither high rainfall nor an acid soil. For them, the near-relative of *Calluna*, the genus *Erica* is the solution. *Erica* as a genus is on an altogether different scale from *Calluna* and embraces something like 700 species; although this is a slightly misleading statistic. Most ericas are South African, staggeringly beautiful but too tender for the British climate. Of the remainder, around ten northern hemisphere species are both hardy and readily enough available to be important garden plants. Some

Can you offer suggestions for a range of primulas for the garden?

There can be few genera of flowering perennials that contain more good garden species and varieties than *Primula*. Some gardeners become quite besotted with them and I do think it's fair to say that there is a primula for every garden and every situation. From the carefully protected habitat of the alpine house where the tiniest and most demanding of species may be cosseted, to the water garden where giant and robust plants vie for attention with other tall border perennials, there is a place for a primula.

Given this huge range, the following selection of *Primulas* is necessarily limited; but it is a personal one of plants that have proved

are, like *Calluna*, acid-loving, but they all differ from *Calluna* in having much more obvious flower colour; the main botanical difference between the two genera is that *Calluna* has its petals largely hidden by the calyx, while *Erica* has the petals not only fully exposed but often inflated and dangling, bell-fashion.

Among the ericas is a small group of species (most notably *Erica carnea* and the hybrid *Erica* x *darleyensis*) that eclipses all others in sheer number of varieties and that are exceptions to the general characteristics of their family in that they are tolerant of alkaline soils. These species are the winter-

relatively easy to grow in my own garden and have given me great pleasure. The secret of continued success is to remember to divide the plants every three years.

My selection of garden primulas (all are dwarf types unless otherwise stated):

Primula alpicola. Moisture-loving; wide range of colours ranging from white to purple with massed tiny flowers at the tops of short stems.

P. auricula (Auricula). Must have very good drainage, be sure to choose only the normal species or border varieties; the show auriculas are only for indoor culture. 'Dusty Miller' is yellow, 'Old Red Dusty Miller' dark red.

P. bulleyana. Moisture-loving, purple flowers on tall spikes.

P. cockburniana. Vivid orange nodding flowers on short spikes.

P. denticulata. Pink and purple 'drumstick' flower heads on tall spikes. 'Alba' is a white form.

P. elatior (Oxlip). Yellow, nodding flowers on tall spikes.

P. florindae. Himalayan cowslip, aptly named, with tall, cowslip-like flowers on very robust stems around midsummer. 75cm/30in.

P. helodoxa. Candelabra form with yellow flowers. 60cm-100cm/24-40in.

P. 'Inverewe'. Candelabra form, orange red 75cm/30cm.

P. japonica. Tall, candelabra form; 'Miller's Crimson' is vivid red, 'Postford White' white with orange-pink eye. 60cm/24in.

P. sikkimensis. Moisture-loving, nodding yellow flowers on tall spikes. 60cm/24in.

P. veris (Cowslip). More or less nodding yellow or orange flowers on short spikes.

P. viallii. Tiny purple flowers in dense spikes, most uncharacteristic of the genus.

P. vulgaris (Primrose). The normal yellow-flowered species is delightful but look out for any of the named double-flowered forms among which the golden 'Sunshine Susie' is lovely. There are also many named single-flowered forms in various colours of which the best known is the deep red-purple 'Wanda'.

flowering heathers, and the flowers that appear at varying times between late autumn and late spring ('winter' is a fairly loose term in the heather business), depending on variety, are their most important attractions. Nonetheless, I grow a good many for their foliage alone as here the variation runs riot and every imaginable shade is obtainable from the palest green through dark greens to yellow, red and some vivid golds, all generally intensifying in the winter.

If there is one drawback to the cultivation of heathers in general, it is one revealed by looking closely at those Scottish mountainsides again. The overall effect is breathtaking but on closer inspection the individual plants are somewhat straggly. Young heathers are neat; older ones aren't. The answer, in gardens, is to renew your plants every few years and in any event trim all of your heathers in the spring; that is, immediately after flowering for the winter-blooming types. Summer-flowering heathers can be trimmed as their flowers fade in the autumn but the dead flower heads look attractive throughout the winter months, especially when covered with a coating of frost.

LEFT: *Primulas not only offer a wide variety in colour, they also give the opportunity for blending with other plants, particularly bulbs.*
See box, pages 104-105.

BELOW: *There are few more welcome sights in the spring than the cheerful golden flowers of aconites, sitting on their green, leafy ruffs.*
See page 109.

Flowering ideas for the coldest months

I HAVE HEARD it suggested that, as gardeners, we have our priorities wrong. We garden for the summer and hope that the rest of the year will take care of itself. In reality, perhaps adopting the opposite approach would do us a great deal more good. British summers are short, even in the most southerly latitudes with the most favoured climates. And there are places in deep Highland glens where only July can be reliably considered free from frost. If we were to design our gardens with winter in mind, surely summer would much more reasonably be taken care of. It's small wonder therefore that I often find myself being asked for suggestions of plants to brighten the coldest months of the year. In large measure, this can be achieved by careful choice of hardy evergreens with attractive foliage shapes and, ideally, variegated patterns. It can be achieved, too, by making use of the less obviously ornamental parts of plants: the bark of trees and shrubs and the dead seed-heads of herbaceous perennials and grasses are among the more obvious. But flowers there can be too and I will offer you my personal choice, a few from within the two important garden plant groups of shrubs and herbaceous perennials that have given me pleasure in the winter months and that should be reliable in nearly all of the country.

My first choice among winter-flowering shrubs is a daphne; *Daphne mezereum* to be precise, a native British plant although not a very common one. It isn't the most spectacular of its genus and it isn't evergreen. But in my garden there is no daphne that combines its hardiness with its reliability for real winter-flowering. And the perfume is well worth the walk to the shrubbery in which I grow it; sweet yet not too heavy, like the better brands of aftershave. The normal species is a lovely plant with rich purple-red flowers but there are good white forms and also a redder variant that I grow.

My second shrub is arguably the most familiar winter-flowering plant of them all. We have, as so often with good things in the garden, to thank a Scotsman for *Jasminum nudiflorum*, the yellow winter-flowering jasmine. Robert Fortune found it in China in 1844. How could we, how did our ancestors, garden without it? The only difficulty with this plant lies in deciding just how to train it, for it is neither climber nor self-supporting shrub. In the wild it scrambles and tumbles. In gardens it should be fixed against a wall; and the sunnier the wall, the more the flowers.

The herbaceous perennial, by definition, is

I fancy having an alpine greenhouse; is this difficult?

In practice, an alpine greenhouse is probably the easiest type of greenhouse to establish and manage. Think of it more as a giant cloche than a greenhouse and you will appreciate its purpose and operation. It serves to protect alpine plants from the worst of the British weather. There should be no heat but plenty of ventilation, ideally

herbaceous and likely in winter to die down to a rootstock. The exceptions are the evergreens of which none are better than those in *Helleborus*. The most obvious winter-flowerer might be thought *Helleborus niger*, although its familiar epithet, Christmas rose, tantalises to disappoint. Some gardeners have *Helleborus niger* in flower at Christmas but they are in the minority and, at least without the benefit of cloche protection, the rest of us have to wait several weeks longer. *Helleborus niger* is a plant of south and central Europe and western Asia but a relative, and another native British plant, can compensate for its shortcomings. One of our two British hellebores is the bear's foot or stinking hellebore, *Helleborus foetidus*, native to alkaline woodland in much of England and Wales but only present I think as a garden escape in Scotland. But little else can match its reliability for winter flowers. The characteristic green dangling bells with purple tips open in late autumn and are still in fine flower by the time that summer beckons.

My second herbaceous plant is a much tinier thing, naturally a species of southern and eastern Europe, but now extensively naturalised in much of Britain. If spring really does have a harbinger (and I have often wondered why other seasons don't have harbingers too), then it must be *Eranthis hyemalis*, the winter aconite. I suppose some gardeners would consider it a bulbous plant as it is from a stubby tuberous rhizome that it grows. But the very fact that planting it as tuberous rhizomes isn't the key to success is why I prefer to call it a herbaceous perennial. Yes, planting rhizomes in the autumn so often leads to disappointing failure. The solution is to buy the thing in leaf and your success is all but assured. Then it will, I hope, spread as it spreads in my garden, by scattering seeds hither and thither to give an ever expanding carpet of gold as those winter flowers with their tiny ruffs of foliage emerge to push away the snow. Winter a colourless time? Not with plants such as these it isn't.

opening vents for the whole length of both sides at bench level. But it is with the benches or staging that the most important constructional feature arises. The staging must be extremely robust and able to withstand a considerable weight. For the ideal way to grow your plants is individually in small terracotta pots sunk to the rim in a bed of small stone chippings. To accommodate the pots, the chippings should be 10-15cm deep. And it will require a very strong bench to support this. The bench must also have provision for free drainage; remember that a major requirement of alpine plants is plenty of water but also the facility for that water to drain away quickly.

THE URBAN SCENE

It's almost impossible to single out one all-embracing characteristic of the Ulster garden. The climate is varied, sometimes kind, sometimes demanding. Some of its gardens are great and spectacular, whilst in its towns will be found some of the finest examples of gardeners making the most of limited space.

The building-site garden

WHETHER IT IS in Cheshire or Sussex, Scotland or Northern Ireland, a home and garden of their own is the goal and dream of many people, young and old. But how often the dream garden turns to nightmare when it is attached to a new house and the raw material is simply the debris that the builders have left behind. Faced with a sea of mud, relieved only by protruding bricks, drainpipes and reject lavatories, how does the would-be gardener make a start?

The first recourse must be to your contract with the builder. Check very carefully to see what provision has been made for reinstatement of the land. Your contract may make provision for replacing topsoil although it should be said that interpretations of 'topsoil' do vary and a depth that satisfies a builder might be very different from that required for gardening. Given that any recently completed building site will be some way from being adequate for immediate gardening, it's important to assess the time that you have available.

If your initial priorities are in the house or at work, and time for gardening is deferred, I would advise you to lay down a temporary lawn. Grass is easily kept tidy and you should use inexpensive turf or seed, simply to cover the plot with vegetation that will go some way towards keeping weeds in check and prevent the soil from blowing away or the area turning into a mud bath. If small children need a place to play, then using playground-grade, chipped bark on a small, defined area would be worthwhile. Then, when time allows, there is no serious alternative to digging over the plot carefully and thoroughly with fork and spade, and

What prickly plants do you suggest to put off intruders from coming into my inner city garden?

It's a sad fact of life that such a question should even arise, let alone be one that I am asked rather frequently. But if intruders do require deterring, there's no doubt that the plant kingdom can do it at least as effectively as wire fencing. The idea of wading through a thicket of berberis to reach their objective will dissuade all except the most toughened ne'er-do-well.

Yes, many of the prickly species of *Berberis* would top my list, and perhaps the prime choice would lie with *Berberis julianae* with its truly wicked, needle-like

removing all debris. Progress will be slow and so it should be. The thoroughness with which you clear the plot at this stage will be repaid many times over in gardening years to come. I'm often asked if it is worth buying in topsoil. If the plot has truly lost all of its original topsoil and the underlying subsoil is unrelieved rock or clay, then it may be. But do remember that a large load of soil won't go very far. A cubic metre of soil weighs approximately 1 tonne and as you need a depth of about 30cm to garden satisfactorily, that tonne will cover an area of only 9sq m.

Having contained the garden and begun to improve the soil, you should then make a list of the features that you hope to include. Do you want a herb garden, a greenhouse and a garden shed? Do you want roses, potentillas, rhododendrons? Are there particular types of tree that have always appealed to you and do you fancy the idea of growing your own fruit and vegetables? Once you have drawn up this basic list, give some thought to the time and money that you are likely to have available over the first few years. And always try to remember that the style of your garden should reflect the style of your house (see pages 33-37).

The next step is to look at the garden from the highest vantage point, usually a bedroom window, and begin to doodle on some sheets of paper. Just jot down where the basic features might fit in and when you reach the point of discovering that there isn't room for everything, discard the more fanciful, time-consuming or costly items. Your main criterion in positioning the features depends on knowing which parts of the garden receive the most sun. This will indicate where to place the sitting-out area, greenhouse and garden pool, all of which must have maximum sunshine. Shrubs, perennials

thorns, bunched in threes. If you want something both beautiful and dramatically spiny, then you need look no further than *Rosa sericea pteracantha*, its thorns enormous and translucent and quite exquisite when seen against the setting sun. If it's a hedge that you want, then hawthorn, holly or gorse will work well; and if you live in a reasonably mild area, then back it with a shrubbery that contains *Colletia hystrix*. It is South American and with strange, thickened, branched stems that end in an elongated tube with a dangerous spine at the tip that will deter an army.

But the selection is vast and if none of my suggestions appeals to you, then turn to your plant catalogue and choose species with specific names like spinosa, spinifera, spinifex, spinescens, spinulifer, spinulosus, horrida, ancylus, ancistrus (like fish-hooks), anguligerus (hooked), arculeatus (prickly), acicularis (needle-like), acanthus (spiny), acerosus (pointed), oxylobus (sharply lobed); there are certainly plenty of suitable plants to choose from.

and pretty well all the other main types of garden plant can then be selected accordingly: sun- or shade-loving. Then a number of other questions will begin to present themselves and I hope you will find some of the answers elsewhere in the book. Is the soil really suitable for those shrubs that you have always wanted? Is your favourite tree really of a size that won't dwarf your house? Some mistakes can be rectified easily but those that relate to garden buildings and trees are the most costly and difficult to correct.

Only when you have a clear idea of what you want should you begin to change things and slowly replace that temporary lawn with more permanent features. Next you should lay down some hard structure in the form of paths and paved areas. And in laying paths, watch the course that people take naturally from one part of the garden to another. Generally, this is not far from the best route for your path. Then plant the largest and slowest-growing plants: trees, followed by shrubs and hedging, each time preparing the planting positions very carefully and thoroughly. Having established the basic framework, you can then gradually move on to creating a permanent, better quality lawn and, eventually, flowerbeds and a vegetable garden.

The container garden

I KNOW THAT container gardening has never been more popular. And I can understand why this should be, for with containers you can produce something instantly appealing, especially in small town or city gardens whether in Belfast or Birmingham, where there are few if any 'proper' garden beds. But containers can also be permanent, long-term features in gardens, both large and small. And you can almost make up your own rules as you go along, although I don't advise using any container less than about 20cm in diameter. With the heat of the summer and plants that are usually shallow-rooted, a container smaller than this will dry out disproportionately quickly and need constant attention.

Window boxes are rather different, however, for the trick here is not to plant anything directly into the box itself. Use as attractive a box as you can afford, provide drainage holes, line it with plastic sheet (also of course with drainage holes), and then place smaller pots containing your plants within. They will appear to be growing *in situ*, but of course can readily be

ABOVE: *A good container collection should include a blend of permanent perennial plants such as clipped shrubs, together with alpines, annuals and other shorter term species.*

replaced during the summer as and when individual plants become exhausted or untidy.

All containers must have drainage holes and a good quality compost. I now use soil-based John Innes No 2 Potting Compost for most of my short-term plantings although I still use a soil-less compost for hanging baskets. I don't trust any bracket with a bowl full of soil at the end of it. Short-term containers should be planted using much the same principles as a circular border or island bed. Start in the centre with your largest plant or plants and gradually work outwards, finishing with trailing types to tumble over the sides. I always keep a few large pelargoniums and fuchsias over the winter to create major central features in my containers in the following spring. Among bedding plants, there are the reliable stand-by species: petunias (including the new trailing 'Surfinia' varieties), lobelias (both cascading and bush types), helichrysum, impatiens, fibrous-rooted begonias, thunbergia, schizanthus, verbena, nepeta, nasturtium and so on. But you can be much more imaginative and use lysimachia (creeping jenny), brachycome (Swan river daisy), diascia, irisine, bidens, scaevola, bacopa and lantana, which looks a delight with its bushy branches carrying masses of flowers of varying colours.

How feasible is it to have a greenhouse in a small town garden?

Perfectly feasible, but don't think in terms of conventional greenhouses. You need a half a greenhouse, better known as a lean-to. This can ideally be

For a herb container, the more obvious candidates are compact 'Curlina' parsley, creeping thymes, variegated sage, creeping pennyroyal mint, chives and golden marjoram. And if herbs, then why not vegetables? Choose small, compact varieties of lettuce, carrots (if the containers are deep enough), beetroot, spinach or tomatoes and whilst you won't be exactly self-sufficient through the summer, you will have a good deal of fun.

Bulbs are obvious container candidates but do be a bit adventurous. I now grow most of my lilies and hybrid tulips in containers. I bring them into view in prominent places in the garden as they come into bloom and move them back again as the flowers fade. The greatest impact is achieved with successions of bulbs. You can achieve this to a degree by planting bulbs of the same variety at different depths but it is even more effective to select plants with different flowering times and plant them in alternate rows and at varying levels. But do remember that even with a soil-based compost, feeding with a liquid fertiliser once a week is essential.

A container for permanent planting can be as big as you choose but once you move into the realm of pots larger than about 60-75cm in diameter, you can't change its position because it will be too heavy to move.

And for the compost, there can be no compromise. For a long-term planting it must be soil-based John Innes No 3 Potting Compost. Simply nothing else has the combination of durability, moisture-retentiveness, fertiliser content and physical support. But nonetheless, container plants, even long-term ones with deep roots, must, positively must, be kept well-watered and also fed at the start of the season with a balanced, preferably organic, fertiliser, such as fish, blood and bone or a proprietary rose feed, and then fed about once a month during the summer with a soluble or liquid feed.

positioned against the wall of your house (the sunnier the wall, the better) and will have the advantage of taking warmth from the house without the need for much costly additional heating. Paint the inner wall white to reflect both warmth and light from the sun, and fit removable staging. In this way, you will be able to raise seedlings in the spring, store pot plants over winter and yet have room for growing tomatoes throughout the summer.

And don't forget that all containers should be raised on small 'feet' or pebbles to improve drainage, help limit frost damage and keep out crawling pests.

And so to the choice of plants, in reality the easiest part of the exercise for I have said many times that any plant can be grown in a container. Shrubs of most types are reliable but do bear in mind that deciduous varieties will look bare once they have shed their leaves. Evergreens, by contrast, can be placed in sheltered spots to protect them from the ravages of winter. Trees make surprisingly good container subjects provided you are careful to check on their ultimate size. My rule of thumb is that a tree that will eventually exceed about 6m might survive, but will seldom look right. Blossom trees are particularly effective and with apples, either ornamental or edible, you have the invaluable option of selecting those that have been grafted on to the rootstock M27 which will give an ultimate height of no more than about 2m.

I would like my small town garden to be like an old-style cottage garden. How is this achieved?

The cottage garden has been described as the only truly indigenous English gardening style. And I suppose if you discount the landscapes of 'Capability' Brown and his kind, this is probably true. Perhaps this is why it is a notion that has returned to popularity of late. Maybe we are all hankering for a return to a golden age, before chemicals and the despoiling of the environment. How the reality differs. The real cottage garden might have had the informality that is now so much in vogue, but it also had chemicals far more noxious than anything we have today. It had weeds, native plants, the odd exotic species, chickens, a pig and people, all in what was often a rather sordid juxtaposition. So by all means let's have a cottage garden feel, but let's not pretend it bears any resemblance to historical reality.

The essential ingredients that you need can be divided into a framework and in-between plantings. For the framework, it is always best if you can start with an existing garden because old and distorted fruit trees are essential. If you must plant young trees, then don't train them but allow them to become irregularly shaped. A few old shrub roses will help create the framework, together with some of the shrubs, including box, holly and lavender, that have graced our gardens for longest. Check with an historical gardening reference book to be sure that you avoid twentieth-century newcomers.

The core of your annual and herbaceous perennial plantings should be of herbs, both culinary and medicinal. And lest you think that this will limit you to thyme, sage and the like, the inclusion of plants that have once had some medicinal value will give you many dozens of very attractive species. But don't be rigid in your plantings. Plant informally, and then, a key to success, allow them to self-seed, weeding out some to keep each species within bounds.

Perhaps the hardest aspect to achieve with any sort of authenticity is in respect of the garden buildings. Clearly, you need somewhere to store your garden equipment, yet a stark, modern, wooden shed is scarcely right. If you already have some form of old, ideally brick or stone garden building, all well and good. If not, then do ensure that any modern building is well covered with trellis which in turn is well embellished with clematis, honeysuckle, rose or other climber. And your greenhouse too should be in keeping. Cottage gardens didn't have aluminium greenhouses; a white painted wooden one must be your goal. It will probably cost more, it will take more maintaining; but then, as I have indicated, cottage gardening really isn't an easy option.

ABOVE: *The informal tangle of peonies, lysimachia, campanulas and tumbling roses help to create a cottage feel in an inner city garden.*

Visiting gardens – great and small

As a Nation, we are too modest by half. There are some areas of endeavour in which we are second to none; and gardening is among them. Yet how often do we show off and display our wares? Someone did once call us a nation of gardeners, although I've long forgotten who it was. But the accuracy of their observation is never more apparent than on a particular occasion sometime in the first few weeks of each year. It's then that our national gardening pre-eminence for once comes to everyone's attention. No, it isn't the Royal Horticultural Society's Chelsea Flower Show in London; it's something far more modest. And although there are certainly many gardens by then already bedecked with early season blossom, it is a publishing event, not a horticultural one that proves the point. The annual emergence of the 'Yellow Books' (*Gardens of England and Wales Open for Charity* and *Gardens of Scotland Open for Charity* has now become an occasion in the garden lover's season that is at least as important as the first crocus, rose or runner bean.

The 'Yellow Books' are the directories of gardens being opened to the public during the year in support of the National Gardens Schemes. A few are great and grand, owned by such institutions as the National Trust or by famous individuals or members of the landed gentry. But most are small and private, adjoining the homes of other gardeners and garden lovers just like you and me. And there are many small gardens in the midst of our bustling towns and cities that are included.

> *Have you some ideas please for non-vigorous climbers to give year-round appeal?*

I learned over the years that 'year-round appeal' is a euphemism for 'evergreen, with flowers, preferably scented'. 'Non-vigorous' is also a euphemism; this time for 'labour-saving, in need of no pruning'. Surprisingly, in view of the large number of ornamental climbers that are now available, these criteria aren't easy to satisfy. For reasons that I explain elsewhere in the book, evergreen plants tend to suffer more than deciduous species in the winter cold. And evergreen climbers, suspended as they are in exposed situations, tend to suffer more than most. I can't, in truth, recommend a completely hardy, evergreen, attractively flowered climber. But the plant that I know that comes closest, is the Chinese *Clematis armandii*, although it can be vigorous and is best given plenty of room to roam. It grows in an exposed spot in my own, rather cold Midland garden and even when young, survived some pretty vicious winters with very little damage. Indeed, the harder the winter, the more it seems to flower in the spring when its lovely masses of cream-white flowers exude a rich perfume to complement the daffodils and tulips that are in bloom nearby. The normal species is good enough but there are two slightly better variants. 'Apple Blossom' has pink buds that open to white flowers, while 'Snowdrift' has a particularly fine fragrance and rather better bronze colouring on the leaves.

After *Clematis armandii*, I think that my votes would go to *Holboellia coriacea*, with its green-white, purple-tinged flowers and *Trachelospermum jasminoides*, with white, jasmine-scented spring flowers, although neither, and especially the *Trachelospermum*, are as tough as the *Clematis armandii*.

Most are open for only one or two days each year so the scheme offers you a very special opportunity to satisfy your curiosity and see what really lies beyond all those garden gates that beckon so invitingly. What could be more tempting than 'a small walled garden adjoining a farmyard in a lovely unspoilt valley with ponds and stream' (that one is in Devon); 'a nineteenth-century garden of 2 hectares with old-fashioned roses and a Chinese pagoda' (that was in Lancashire) or even (from Kent), a raised vegetable garden, purpose-built for a disabled owner around a small semi-detached house.

The 'Yellow Book' is not a lavish, glossily illustrated publication and I hope it never becomes one. But within its pages are the keys to one of our greatest national treasures: our garden know-how. Because what is so uniquely important about the scheme is that it gives you access to the most wonderful gardening school available to everyone all over the country. If the best way to learn about gardening is to do it and to make mistakes, the next best way is to talk to fellow gardeners and see how they have tackled particular problems and observe their successes and failures. There is a limit to what ten or even a hundred visits to Stourhead (Wiltshire), Exbury (Hampshire) or Bodnant (Gwynedd) can teach you about the planning and maintenance of your own small plot in Inner London, on the Yorkshire hills or on a housing development outside Glasgow. And above all, I find that it is the matter of scale that is the greatest problem in bringing home ideas.

Great and famous gardens tend to be big gardens. Whilst gardens such as Sissinghurst (Kent) and Hidcote (Gloucestershire) are subdivided into compartments or 'rooms', they are also compartments of like plants. The

ABOVE: *The private gardens open under the 'Yellow Book' scheme offer you a special glimpse into the untold wealth of British gardening.*

red border of Hidcote and the white garden of Sissinghurst might be both beautiful and clever but they are of little practical assistance to someone wanting a little of everything, including fruit and vegetables, in a small garden plot. As I've said many times, gardening is a personal matter. What is right for one person may be wrong for another, even if horticulturally it is sound enough. But see enough private gardens and you will gain ideas. Talk to fellow gardeners and you will appreciate how your problems and quandaries aren't unique. And you will come away, not disheartened as you might in professional gardening company, but encouraged to try yourself.

The clematis

CLEMATIS MAY NOT carry the epithet Queen of the Climbers (that is reserved for wisteria) but there is no denying which is the most popular. And I don't think any climber offers better value for a small town garden. Questions and requests for advice on clematis must outnumber those for all other climbing plants by about ten to one. And why not, for there is a plant among the group for pretty well every garden and pretty well every position. All it needs is for more gardeners to appreciate the full scope of the genus.

Unexpectedly, I always feel, *Clematis* belongs to the buttercup family, the Ranunculaceae. Unexpectedly too, the glorious flower colour comes not from petals which are rudimentary, but from sepals. The genus is a big one, embracing some 200 species, and occurs throughout temperate parts of the world. It is worth remembering however that 'temperate' can mean warm temperate and there are some clematis too tender to grow outdoors in our climate. Some species however are rather variable and ever since their cultivation began, gardeners have made selections and crosses to produce the complex hybrids that are some of today's most popular garden forms. So the 200 species are swollen in number by around 400 varieties.

LEFT: *If you really want a spectacular display of clematis, look no further than the numerous varieties of* Clematis montana. *But do remember to position them with care; they are the most vigorous of all the many types of clematis.*

We have only one native British clematis in the shape of the old man's beard, *Clematis vitalba*, a very common plant that festoons hedgerows with its exuberant garlands and swags, almost anywhere that the soil isn't seriously acidic. No doubt it was grown in early gardens, where it was joined during the sixteenth century by several European species, most notably the beautiful Spanish *Clematis viticella*, the parent of numerous modern varieties. Apart from the yellow, bell-flowered *Clematis orientalis*, the next important influx of new blood came in the late eighteenth and early nineteenth centuries. One of my own personal favourites, the spring-flowering *Clematis alpina*, was European but it was the opening up of China that has enabled us to grow and breed from such important species as *Clematis florida*, *Clematis lanuginosa*, *Clematis patens* and the wonderful evergreen *Clematis armandii* (see box, pages 120-121).

It is a disappointment to me that few true species are grown in gardens today. Clematis now tends to mean the large, summer-flowering hybrids and 'Nelly Moser', 'Jackmanii' and 'Perle d'Azur' have almost become by-words for clematis in many gardeners' thinking. I have no argument with this but by being rather more catholic in their selection, they could have clematis in flower for about nine months of the year.

My clematis season begins in April with the exquisitely fragrant *Clematis armandii* and one or more of the *Clematis alpina* varieties; the double flowered 'White Moth' or the large pendant blue bells of 'Frances Rivis'. They are soon followed by a selection from the extremely vigorous *Clematis montana*. These are plants to position with care, so rampant are they, but forced to select just one, it would be the fragrant, pink 'Elizabeth'. If you love the montanas but don't really have room, then be introduced to another Chinese species in

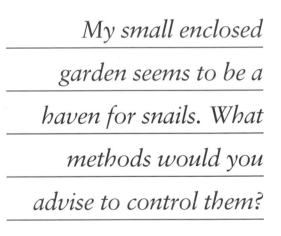

My small enclosed garden seems to be a haven for snails. What methods would you advise to control them?

Snails tend to be particularly troublesome in small town gardens as these types of gardens and their boundary walls in particular are often clothed with climbing plants. In and among these, the snails hide and breed. Remove ivy and similar climbers from the walls and snails

Clematis chrysocoma which is similar but more restrained. 'Continuity' is its best form.

We move into early summer with some of the large-flowered hybrids. The rich, deep purple-flowered, 'The President', takes pride of place among them in my garden, largely because it is unusual in the group in continuing to bloom for much of the summer. But others of distinction among early-flowering hybrids are 'Dr Ruppel', one of a number of varieties with pronounced stripes or bars on the flowers; 'Nelly Moser' herself, as much as anything for the size and quantity of her mauve and pink blooms, and the beautiful, sumptuous white 'Marie Boisselot'. Among the later-flowering hybrids too are some much-loved varieties: the 'Jackmanii' group, the mauve pink 'Hagley Hybrid' and 'Perle d'Azur', pale blue and, I am told by nurserymen and garden centres, the biggest-selling clematis of them all.

Comes late summer and the plant that I think is my favourite of them all, is decorating the trellis at the end of my kitchen garden. The *Clematis viticella* hybrid 'Mme Julia Correvon' just asks to be allowed to hang down, either from an artificial support or from the branches of a low tree. Her rich, velvety, deep red flowers are perfect companions for later-flowering pink or white shrub roses.

The clematis flowering season then closes with a collection of the yellowish flowered Oriental species and their derivatives. Among the finest is 'Bill Mackenzie' with very large yellow bells and 'Orange Peel' appropriately named for its remarkable rich yellow-orange flowers and thickened sepals. All are fairly vigorous and should be allowed to scramble through trees. But do note that even when the official flowering season closes there is still much to admire. For the flowers are followed by lovely feathery seedheads produced by most of the species and some of the hybrids and they

will fall out in their hundreds. But removing the climbers isn't a realistic option in gardens such as these and you can only resort to crude control. Chemical slug baits will kill snails too (although the nematode-based biological controls generally won't), and if you have pets or concerns about wildlife, use liquid baits and/or conceal them beneath pieces of tile or other covers for protection. Traps in the form of glass jars sunk to their rim and baited with beer will catch snails as well as slugs but probably the best and most reliable method of all is to catch the creatures by hand. Go out after dark (snails are nocturnal creatures) and hand-pick them into a bucket for disposal later. It may seem unpleasant but you can always wear gloves; and, as I often remind people, unlike slugs, snails do have a handle.

How effective and reliable are winter hanging baskets?

Very effective, especially in sheltered gardens, such as town gardens tend to be. The only real problems arise in very cold and windy positions where the plants will inevitably suffer. But do be aware that the choice of plants suitable for winter baskets is much more limited than in summer; and, most importantly, remember that they won't put on much growth. Put seedlings into a summer basket and within weeks the basket will be full. In winter, the plants will remain more or less the same size so it's essential to select ones that are big enough, and use sufficient of them to fill the basket from the beginning.

Although less watering is needed in winter, a basket with a good cover of vegetation will dry out, even in rainy weather, so do keep a close eye on the compost. But because the plants grow so little, feeding is much less important and two or three applications of a liquid feed through the winter months will be sufficient.

Among the plants that are well worth growing and reliable are winter-flowering heathers, dwarf or baby conifers, tolmeia, winter-flowering pansies (nothing can hold a candle to them for their beautiful winter flower colour), small spring bulbs such as miniature crocus, vinca, small-leaved ivies, lamiums and ajuga.

should be left on the plants through the winter: they look delightful when decorated with a silvery coating of frost.

Plant clematis in any good, well-drained soil, ideally slightly alkaline or amended with a dressing of lime. Feed them through the summer and prune them in the spring; and, as with most flowering shrubs, follow the rule that the later in the year the flowers form, the harder should the plants be pruned. Cut back and remove any that show signs of wilt, at any time.

ABOVE: *Planted with a selection of differently textured evergreens, a hanging basket perks up dull grey winter days.*

Choosing the hard landscape

GARDENING IS PRINCIPALLY, of course, about plants, but whether your garden is in the town, a city or in the countryside the framework within which the plants grow is equally important. There are situations where the physical environment occupies an even greater part of the total area, than do the plants. It is a matter of achieving the correct balance for your own particular garden style, and of using the most appropriate materials. As with most other aspects of gardening, the final choice is likely to be dictated by cost, but in recent years there have been significant developments in the manufacture of excellent substitutes for pretty well all expensive original landscape materials.

Gravel and stone chips are, for me, among the most useful of all the hard landscaping materials and I use them extensively in my own garden. They are all relatively low cost, relatively easy to lay (porous landscaping fabric should be put down first to suppress weed growth) and have the inestimable merit of easily going around corners and into crevices. They are

BELOW: Gravel is perhaps the most versatile of all material for covering the ground. You can walk on it, stand containers on it and, most effectively, grow plants through it.

now available in many different grades and colours. Grits are prepared from crushed rock and have angular particles. They tend to be more expensive but can be compacted when heavy-rolled, while gravels, with rounded particles, remain loose but give that appealing crunching sound when walked on. The loose types of gravel are among the cheapest of all landscaping materials but they do need to be confined by raised edges to prevent them from spilling onto lawns. They are always attractive but are less practical where they are likely to be walked on with muddy boots. In addition to areas for walking on, gravel and chippings can be used most effectively to produce gardens or beds in which they comprise a substantial part of the ornamental area, for most plants will happily grow through them. The lovely garden of designer John Brookes at Denmans in Sussex is a wonderful example of this type of planting.

Slabs will be the natural choice for many paths and larger areas of hard landscaping but must be chosen with care and thought. In order to preserve the natural landscape, new slabs can only be bought from approved quarries while even second-hand slabs of genuine York or other stone, while beautiful in appearance, have become almost prohibitively

How can I create a miniature water garden?

Much the best way is to have a tub garden, using an old wooden half-barrel. It's important to use a real half-barrel, not one made up for garden use, as in the genuine article, the planks swell to become water-tight. The made-up tubs for containing plants will always leak. Don't be too ambitious with your plantings however.

expensive. Nonetheless, some quite excellent artificial substitutes made of concrete or reconstituted stone are now available at a small fraction of the originals' cost. Basic, plain concrete slabs, however, should be employed with great caution as their impact is almost impossible to soften and their only real place is in a very formal setting when the best quality should be used. Slabs should be laid on sand or dry-set onto cement but not pointed. Instead, fill the gaps with compost and mat-forming plants such as thymes and low-growing dianthus that are tolerant of being trodden on. They will root happily, softening the effect and adding colour and perfume. Slabs set in grass should be slightly below the level of the lawn, making it easy for the mower to pass over the top of the slab.

Although bricks look correct and attractive when used for paving in some gardens, particularly where the house itself is built of brick, they are out of place in others. Old bricks can be obtained fairly easily, but they often require fastidious cleaning and are usually unsuitable for paving since they soon tend to crumble. Modern 'engineering' bricks are perfectly acceptable, especially if they can be obtained second-hand and weathered. Nonetheless, I've been extremely impressed with some of the less expensive modern replica bricks and I don't think that in any other area of landscaping material have the improvements been so great. Other types of paving blocks exist in a vast range of colours, sizes and textures. Some simulate natural materials, others are unashamedly artificial. Most are expensive, many prohibitively so, for all except the smallest of areas. Stone cobbles, granite sets and tiles, both original and replica, can all have a place in the garden. Always try to see a sample area laid, for the end result can be surprisingly different from the appearance of individual pieces.

Wood can be used for paving and is less widely seen than it might be. Short lengths of hardwood trunks, set vertically, can produce an extremely pleasing appearance, a fact known to the gardeners of Japan for centuries. Unfortunately, such areas are better looked at than walked on, for they can be extremely slippery when wet. Large fragments of shredded bark, similar to those used for mulching, can also make attractive and functional paths.

Although invaluable when in the form of replica slabs, concrete used fresh is a dismal material, providing unrelieved monotony on patios. It is perhaps slightly more acceptable in restricted form as paths, or where the surface is roughened by adding coarse gravel. Apart from cheapness, it has few other merits and is surpassed, among materials to avoid, only by tarmac. Nothing ruins the appearance of any garden as much as a boring expanse of this dreadful black material, unless it is tarmac to which some

Place a few half-bricks in the tub to become ledges to hold the planting baskets. Choose one miniature water lily (*Nymphaea tetragona*, also sold as 'Pygmaea Alba', makes a good choice), a couple of non-vigorous marginal plants such as spearwort (*Ranunculus flammula*) or one of the small varieties of *Iris laevigata*, a non-vigorous submerged oxygenating plant such as *Myriophyllum species*, a few snails and two small goldfish. Your tub garden will give you hours of pleasure but do be thorough in removing dead leaves and other debris promptly.

coloured paint has been applied. Please resist the persuasive powers of people who arrive uninvited at your door, just happening to have a load of steaming tar with them, and offer to 'do' your drive.

Garden ornaments

THERE IS VERY MUCH more to a garden than its plants. There's even more to a garden than the hard landscaping that I've discussed (see pages 126-129). I've often stressed the personal nature of gardens; how gardening is as much about the people who create the gardens as it is about plants and there's no area of the subject in which this is more positively displayed than garden ornamentation. Should you, can you, must you have ornaments in your garden? And, if so, what is acceptable and what not? How do you make a choice from the extensive range that stretches from classical lead goddesses to modern plastic gnomes? These are choices of especial importance in small town gardens where every ingredient is so much more obvious.

I am a self-confessed garden decorator. I do believe that appropriately chosen statuary or other ornament enhances rather than detracts from the surrounding plants. And it is indeed such non-living elements that convey most of the immediate impression of time, period and style. Even before a gardener sows the first seed or plants the first plant, he or she can have progressed a long way towards giving the garden its characteristic stamp of style that it will grow into.

What are your suggestions for the best small garden tree?

Everyone wants to plant a tree but most people have small gardens. In consequence, some unfortunate and sometimes costly mistakes are made. Remember that it's very much easier to plant a young tree than to remove a big one some years later when it threatens house and neighbourhood. So choose carefully. I can't

expect that what appeals to me will necessarily appeal to everyone else but the following trees will all function well and be most unlikely to cause trouble. But check the ultimate height of your chosen tree and as a rule of thumb, don't plant nearer to the house than one and a half times this distance. This will soon tell you if your garden is big enough for your selection:

Acer palmatum 'Senkaki' (Japanese maple). For autumn leaf colour.

Acer capillipes (Snake-bark maple)

Betula utilis (White barked birch)

Magnolia grandiflora 'Goliath' (Evergreen magnolia)

Magnolia stellata (Star magnolia)

Malus 'Golden Hornet'. Flowering crab apple with small, golden fruit.

Prunus sargentii. The best flowering cherry.

Prunus serrula (Tibetan cherry). Has shiny copper coloured bark.

Robinia pseudoacacia 'Frisia'. False acacia with golden yellow foliage.

Salix 'Erythroflexuosa' (Twisted willow). Try to obtain one of the forms with red-orange bark.

LEFT: *The ornamental crab apple 'Golden Hornet' is probably the prettiest among a very attractive group of fruiting trees for autumn colour.*

RIGHT: *Garden statuary need be neither large nor expensive; but it should be appropriate in both subject and colour to its surroundings.*

Nonetheless, if there is one message to convey when choosing statuary and other ornaments, it is to be restrained and to take your time. Even in a relatively large garden, one carefully selected object, placed at a focal point, can be immeasurably more dramatic than dozens of smaller ones. It is remarkable how effective a statue can be at taking your eye in a particular direction. If you have a prominently-sited garden pool, place a figure in the water; or use a statue as an integral part of the fountain for extra focal effect.

When looking for a statue, you will at first be bewildered by the choice, not only in pattern but also in quality and in the materials used. Genuine old stone or lead statues are almost prohibitively expensive but modern reproductions are now so good that they make perfectly acceptable alternatives. And new statues need not look new; paint the surface either with milk or with a mixture of cow manure and water to encourage the growth of algae and lichens.

I have trouble with neighbourhood cats visiting my garden; how can I dissuade them?

The only infallible method that I know is to have a cat of your own. If this doesn't appeal or is impractical, you can try exclusion, dissuasion or repelling.

Exclusion only works if your garden is totally surrounded by a wall or fence over

I've mentioned how the choice of statue can dictate the style that your garden reflects. And even replicas of older patterns aren't themselves a recent invention. Urns in stone, reconstituted stone, terracotta or cast iron were popular in the Victorian period and ornaments in an even older formal Italian style were especially sought after in the second half of the nineteenth century. Lead has been used since Roman times for water containers but whilst an original old cistern with an embossed date would make an admirable feature for a courtyard garden, its likely price today will put it out of most gardeners' budgets.

Where lead made another appearance however was in some well-head pumps, which were made either entirely of cast iron or encased in a wooden box with lead covering. These still exist in many gardens dating from the Victorian period but if your garden already has a well, an original pump for it is certainly worth seeking, especially if it is possible to find one

which the cat must climb. Attaching a single strand of wire approximately 2cm above the top of the barrier will prevent the cats from being able to balance on top and will be pretty effective. Dissuasion means placing prickly twigs or proprietary plastic 'prickle mats' among your plants, and especially on newly dug soil. Repelling means the use of chemical repellents, none of which I have found very effective, or using one of the electronic devices sold for the purpose and which are operated either by battery or low voltage transformer and emit a high frequency sound, inaudible to us but apparently very unappealing to cats. These seem to work fairly well.

in working order. As an alternative, modern cast iron well-pumps in nineteenth-century style can be obtained quite cheaply. It should go without saying that the fairy-story well-heads with painted buckets whose inspiration derives principally from Walt Disney are as out of place in the centre of a lawn or a flower bed (which is where they are normally to be found) as they would be over a real well.

In addition there are several types of ornament, popular in gardens today, which although seemingly ancient, are merely modern fancies. The bird bath is essentially a twentieth-century creation that has arrived hand in hand with our increased concern for wildlife. Our ancestors weren't so concerned with such things and their birds did their bathing elsewhere. The sundial certainly dates from an earlier age, when men really used them to tell the time, although during the nineteenth century, mechanical things were what gardeners really wanted and the sundial faded from appeal. The staddle stone is an apparently indispensable, but functionally useless, object in many a garden today. Both originals and replicas are available at very high prices but their use as garden ornaments is entirely modern and their real purpose was to support grain stores clear of the ground and protect them from rats.

Furniture is an important garden feature, in an aesthetic as well as a functional sense and represents one aspect of period gardening for which accurate reproductions are readily available. Several dozens of the many different styles of historical garden chair and table are now produced, either in wood or in cast iron. They mimic designs from Victorian and Regency times and combine the creation of a period feel with a very important functionality. For I've also always believed that every garden should have plenty of places of sit. Gardening is only partly about creating something; it's also about sitting down to admire it.

TREES, SHRUBS & WOODLANDS

Britain is no longer a wooded land,
although trees remain deeply planted in
our national psyche. And whilst the
English oak might be the age-old symbol
of a country's spirit, the beechwoods of
the Chilterns seem to offer as tantalising
a glimpse of a lost landscape as can
still be found. Even on a small scale, trees
can bring some of this spirit into your
own garden.

Understanding how woodlands work

I'VE ALWAYS BELIEVED that gardeners can learn most about gardening by lifting their eyes from their own plot to look out through the garden gate, and this holds good whether you have the Chiltern beechwoods or New Forest nearby. Nature is a fine and experienced tutor whose instruction can be manifest in any number of ways. At its most simple, it can mean discovering which types of plant are most suitable for your garden soil. At a wider level, it can mean discovering the way to create a particular type of planting. You see, we tend to forget that garden beds, borders, shrubberies and other garden features are simply replicas of some natural plant association. And I don't think that there is any better example of this than that most fascinating of natural plant habitats – a woodland. Seeing how a natural woodland works can tell you a good deal about how to use trees and shrubs in your garden.

It is important however to look at what passes most closely for a natural wood, not a recent planting. Although there are around 2,000,000 hectares of woodland in Britain, almost none of it is part of the ancient forest that once covered a large proportion of these islands. Most of the woodland that you will see today has been planted in relatively recent history, either for timber or for game cover. The two most important survivors of the older plantings are the medieval New Forest in Hampshire and the Forest of Dean in Gloucestershire. In some areas, moreover, old plantings or more restricted areas of natural woodland have been felled wholesale in times of national need, and the beechwoods of the Chilterns, for example, are the results of natural regeneration. The extensive areas of coniferous forest in Britain today are almost entirely the results of recent planting for timber and paper by the Forestry Commission and by private landowners. To see truly old coniferous woodland, you must

Is there a rule of thumb for the pruning of climbers?

There are several rules of thumb for pruning any plant; and climbers are no more than elongated shrubs. First, if in doubt, don't. You will do no serious harm by leaving a plant unpruned; at worst, its flowering or other performance may

visit the Black Wood of Rannoch, a survivor of the primeval Caledonian pine forest.

But a natural wood isn't a random collection of plants that happen to be growing in the same place through some accident of history. It's a rather precisely structured collection of individuals and species brought together because of a combination of climate and soil. And it wasn't created at a single moment, but has evolved over a period of years during which some species have tried and failed to grow while others have been replaced as the environment itself changed. Woods, like all other groups of plants, including gardens, aren't static. As plants grow and become bigger, they change their immediate vicinity. Deciduous plants shed their leaves, adding to the organic matter in the soil and so changing the soil's make-up. And trees grow taller and so cut out increasingly more of the sunlight. Those plants that were happy to grow alongside a young tree in the full sunshine therefore find things less to their liking. Their place is taken by species more tolerant of shade.

But the end result is that once the trees, the biggest and tallest plants, have reached their full height, the changes become less, and the type and combination of species growing beneath them stabilises. In a mature wood, therefore, there will be more or less of several layers: the trees themselves, beneath them big shrubs, beneath them smaller shrubs and big herbaceous plants, beneath them, in turn, smaller herbaceous plants and finally, low-growing, ground-cover perennials, bulbs and annuals.

A garden wood or shrubbery is no different in essential structure except that we have created it at a stroke. So, if we plant annuals beneath shrubs or beneath trees, surely success is assured. Unfortunately, this isn't so. Trees are, and expect to be, the tallest members of any plant grouping and it matters little what types of plant grow beneath. The same isn't true of the smaller plants themselves. Whilst

suffer but this is something that can always be corrected later when the facts have been checked. Whilst most plants will recover from bad or unnecessary pruning, however, others may suffer long-term harm, generally by decay entering through the pruning cuts or the plant being unable to produce new growth from old wood. But the second and more general rule of thumb is to prune as soon as possible after flowering; and the later in the year that the plant flowers, the harder should you prune. There are a few exceptions to this but it works well with pretty well all climbers, including clematis.

some shrubs and some annuals (although rather few of the latter) do have their natural home in the deep shade of bigger things, others don't. Rhododendrons, camellias and mahonias, for example, will grow contentedly in the shade and fare less well in full sun, simply because this is the type of habitat in which they grow naturally. It doesn't much matter that the trees providing shade for them in your garden are very different from those that are their companions in the wild. By contrast, potentillas and gorse, whilst also undoubtedly shrubs, are not naturally plants of the woodland. They grow out in the open, in the full sun, and so these are the conditions they must have in gardens. Plant them at the edges of the shaded areas or in openings in the tree canopy.

Maples

NO ONE GROUP of trees more conjures up the appeal and beauty of autumn colour than the maples. If you visit any area of planted woodland or any of the great national arboreta (see pages 141-147) in autumn, it is beech among the native trees and the maples among the exotics that elicit

the most admiration. And yet a relatively small range of maples contributes to our gardens, and many of those popularly used aren't always the best for ornamental value, and not all have autumn colour as their primary appeal.

The maple genus, *Acer*, encompasses around 150 species and surprisingly, for a genus so highly regarded for its autumn colour, there are some evergreens among them. As a genus, their distribution is wide, covering both North and South America, Europe and Asia. Sadly however, the European species are not by and large of great ornamental merit. Our native British field maple, *Acer campestre,* is too large for gardens and has no real redeeming features other than as a hedgerow tree, and the introduced sycamore, *Acer pseudoplatanus* (other than in the form 'Brilliantissimum', possibly) is at best a useful plant to stabilise sand dunes and at worst a weedy, self-seeding nuisance. Only the Norway maple, *Acer platanoides*, in its purple-leaved forms like 'Crimson King', can be called at all ornamental. Indeed Europe as a whole is poorly supplied with native maples. *Acer opalus*, the Italian maple, and *Acer trautvetteri* from further east are not much improvement on the sycamore. *Acer heldreichii*, from the Balkans, is a big tree although quite pretty as the leaves unfold, while *Acer tataricum* and *Acer monspessulanum* from southern Europe have leaves most untypical of the maples as a whole.

It's to North America and especially the Far East that we must turn for the gems of the maple world. Interestingly, however, the maples that prove such a magnetic attraction for visitors to New England and other parts of North America in the autumn, rarely offer anything like the same spectacular colours in Europe. Such species as the red maple, *Acer rubrum*, the famous sugar maple of Canada, *Acer saccharum*, and the silver maple, *Acer saccharinum*, seem only to perform to their best when warm autumn days are combined with chilly nights. In Britain, days and nights become chilly at the same time.

Both for colour and other features too, Japanese maples supply the most wonderful selection. *Acer palmatum* has given rise to some incredible varieties, long-known and grown as important and integral features of Japanese gardens. Among the huge number of varieties, most with Japanese names, I must pick out 'Inaba-Shidare', 'Linearilobum', 'Osakazuki', 'Seiryû' and 'Shaina'; for their combination of leaf shape, spring and summer leaf colour and autumn fire. But *Acer palmatum* has also spawned a variety called *dissectum* from which, in turn, a number of forms have been selected. Their unifying characteristic is a finely dissected, almost filigree leaf and this, combined with very slow growth rate and incredible autumn colour, gives them a special appeal. Because they must be propagated by grafting and because demand always outstrips supply, they are never cheap. But they are not difficult to grow and if your soil is wet and/or your garden windy, neither to

Do I *need* permission to cut down a garden tree?

It depends where you live, how large the tree is, what type of tree it is, and if it is dead. Generally speaking, you may cut down a dead, dying or dangerous tree without asking anyone (although be aware that there may be dispute over what constitutes 'dying'). If the tree is alive and well, it may have one of two types of legal protection. A fine, specimen tree may be protected by a Tree Preservation Order, (generally shortened to TPO) taken out by a local authority whose permission will be needed before the tree may be pruned, let alone felled. You may be unaware of an existing preservation order on one of your trees, so it's wise to check. If an authority proposes to take out a new preservation order, they will inform you of this. Even if a tree is not protected individually, it will automatically acquire protection if you live in a designated Conservation Area and if it has a trunk diameter of more than 7.5cm at a height of 1.5m above ground level. In such circumstances, you are obliged to inform the local authority of your intentions and obtain their permission; and even if they agree to your actions, they may still require you to replace any tree that enjoys legal protection. But always, if in any doubt, ask first.

their liking, then growing one, Japanese-style, in a container in a sheltered spot, will give you a plant to be treasured.

Acer japonicum is by no means the only beautiful Oriental foliage maple and at the risk of merely cataloguing, I would commend, among many others, *Acer shirasawanum* 'Aureum' with butter-yellow leaves, the rare but exquisitely lovely Korean *Acer pseudosieboldianum*, with reds and oranges to match no other, and *Acer japonicum* (the 'other' Japanese maple) in its variety 'Vitifolium' for reds, purples and golds.

But finally, for a combination of autumn leaf brilliance and the most beautifully textured bark, may I introduce you to another group within this extraordinary genus. The appropriately named snake-barked maples are mainly Oriental; small trees with vertical irregular patterning on the bark, reminiscent to some people of a snake's skin, but with glorious leaf colours too. Among a very lovely group, the one that graces one of my own lawns, *Acer grosseri* var. *hersii* would be my choice. And then, last of all, of great beauty in autumn, but famed above all for its most extraordinary peeling bark, is one of Ernest Wilson's first and most precious 'captures' on his plant collecting journeys to China: the paper-barked maple, *Acer griseum*.

Arboreta

ARBORETUM: A PLACE where trees are cultivated, from the Latin *arbor*, a tree. It's a nineteenth-century word and, interestingly, it was the name used for the first municipal park in Britain, which opened in Derby in 1840. Early public parks tended to be small collections of trees so this made sense. Only when carpet bedding and lavish aspects of Victorian horticulture took over did the name arboretum pass from favour for such places.

But it continued elsewhere and many a stately house had its arboretum, often separate from the remainder of the garden. In a few instances, nonetheless, the arboretum was the garden and the collection of trees an entity in itself.

As a nation, we have long had a love of trees and although our own country doesn't now have the densely wooded natural landscape of earlier centuries, this has been amply compensated by the huge numbers of species introduced by plant collectors. From elsewhere in Europe, China and North America especially have come both deciduous and evergreen trees by the score. And by good fortune, this influx began in the eighteenth century, when the gardening style that has been described as our only truly indigenous horticultural creation came to the fore. The landscape movement of Lancelot 'Capability' Brown and his kind was essentially the creation of huge gardens of grass and trees. Its exponents greeted every new woody species that came along with unmitigated enthusiasm.

Not all ornamental trees were planted in arboreta. A few years ago, that great connoisseur of trees, the late Alan Mitchell, listed around 500 places in Britain where notable tree specimens can be seen. Some are small collections, some are gardens with trees dotted around (when they may be called a woodland

RIGHT: *The pastoral scene at Westonbirt is given a vivid splash of yellow with the autumnal foliage of* Acer cappadocicum.

garden if the trees are particularly numerous, as at Sheffield Park in Sussex), some are isolated individuals. But there are also a few outstanding large collections solely of trees and shrubs that can be described as proper arboreta.

The most famous of all arboreta in Britain must be Westonbirt in Gloucestershire, one of the great glories of any English autumn. The collection was begun in 1829 by Robert Holford as an extension to the park that surrounded Westonbirt House (now a well-known school). The three oldest avenues of trees were aligned with respect to the house but the planting soon spread far beyond them. The outstanding feature of Westonbirt today is the Acer collection, largely the work of Robert Holford's son, Sir George Holford, towards the end of the nineteenth and early in the twentieth century. He also planted extensive rhododendron collections, so adding a spring appeal to match the autumn. More recently, there has been extensive planting of willows and Westonbirt, now in the ownership of the Forestry Commission, has one of the National Collections of *Salix*. Like most great plant collections, varieties that originated there perpetuate the name and one of the finest forms of the red-barked dogwood, *Cornus alba,* is known as 'Westonbirt'.

There is a danger that any comprehensive collection of one type of plant can be little more than a living catalogue. And this is a criticism that has been levelled at the Hillier Arboretum in Hampshire. Certainly, there are more imaginatively arranged arboreta, but as the plantings reach maturity the collection at Hilliers takes on an increasing aesthetic appeal. And there's never been any denying its compre-

Is there anything that can be done to prevent honey fungus from appearing or spreading in my garden?

Although most gardeners are terrified at the thought of honey fungus, it's usually only a problem in gardens that have once been woodland or orchard, or have a similar long history of containing deciduous trees. For the fungus usually gains a foothold through the cut surface of old stumps, spreading to healthy trees nearby by means of dark strands, like bootlaces. If a tree or shrub appears to be dying or to have been killed by honey fungus attack, the entire stump should be uprooted and disposed of, preferably by burning, together with as much of the root system as possible. Dig as large a hole as practicable and dump the soil in a part of the garden well away from other trees and shrubs. It's easiest to dig a second hole in the vegetable garden, and swap the soil between the two. The hole and surrounding infected area may be drenched with a proprietary control solution, which

hensiveness and horticultural value. The late Sir Harold Hillier bought Jermyns House near Romsey in 1953 and spent the next 20 years planting his collection, as an adjunct to the world famous family nursery. He donated the collection to Hampshire County Council in 1978. It now comprises in excess of 10,000 species and varieties planted over 64 hectares. If it's the maples that are the shining glory of Westonbirt, it must be the rhododendrons, azaleas, camellias and other acid-soil plants that are the enduring memory of Hillier. Nonetheless, the fact that there are ten National Collections here, and rhododendron isn't even included, is ample testimony to its importance and richness.

An offspring from the arboretum proper that arose during the nineteenth century was the pinetum, a collection not simply of pines but of conifers generally. Oddly, although the general advice is that deciduous trees are better in a polluted atmosphere (shedding their leaves in autumn, they are able to start afresh each year), conifers did thrive remarkably well in the dirty air close to nineteenth-century towns and cities. James Bateman had a pinetum at Biddulph Grange close to the then smoky Stoke-on-Trent. But the greatest collection must be that in the much cleaner air at the appropriately titled National Pinetum at Bedgebury in Kent. Like Westonbirt, this is owned by the Forestry Commission and as its main plantings were made in the mid-1920s, there are some truly magnificent mature specimens. Its collection of hardy conifer species and their varieties is the finest in the world and despite losses through storms and gales, still all

may have some effect in killing the bootlace strands in the soil, although it won't cure an already diseased tree. The affected site shouldn't be replanted for at least one year and preferably two.

If honey fungus is known to be present in a neighbour's garden, install a physical barrier to the bootlace strands. Dig a vertical slit trench, 1m deep close to the garden boundary, and in it bury vertically a rigid plastic sheet. A similar slit trench, containing a plastic barrier dug in a circle around a stump known to be diseased, is sometimes effective in preventing further spread of honey fungus in a newly infested garden. Once honey fungus is present, even if diseased stumps can be removed, any major new plantings should be with the more resistant tree and shrub species and never with those known to be highly susceptible:

Highly susceptible trees: apple, birch, cedar, cypress, lilac, pine, privet, walnut and willow.

Moderately resistant trees: ash, beech, box, clematis, Douglas fir, elaeagnus, hawthorn, holly, ivy, larch, laurel, lime, mahonia, robinia, silver fir, sumac, tamarisk, tree of heaven (*Ailanthus altissima*) and yew.

What makes the best all round garden hedge?

A garden hedge serves several purposes. It marks your boundary, it keeps out people and animals, it offers privacy, it acts as a windbreak, it provides a backdrop to other garden plants and features, and it may be an attractive thing in its own right. But it is very difficult for any hedge to achieve all of these objectives equally well and at all times of the year. Some of the best screens, like privet and cypresses, are depressingly dull. Some of the prettiest, like berberis, are too insubstantial to provide privacy or, like escallonia, only really effective in milder areas. Some of the best in most respects are deciduous and so offer much less in winter. On balance, and forced to choose a hedge for every season and every garden, I would have to opt for yew – evergreen, dense, able to be shaped, and a wonderful background although a little sombre for some; and beech – lighter, brighter, less dense than yew, not as good as a backdrop, prone to aphids, deciduous although retaining its dead leaves through the winter and so still offering screening and protection.

but comprehensive. If you want to see what a particular species will look like in your garden in 10 or 20 years time, you should pay a visit. For whilst they are beautiful to behold, the mistakes that could be avoided by seeing what would happen if big trees are put in small gardens would alone repay the entrance fee.

LEFT: *It's inescapable: yew is the finest hedging plant of all; and the widespread belief that it is slow-growing is completely misplaced.*

The shrub legacy of South America

I'M NOT SURE whom I blame but there's no doubt that in recent years gardeners have become obsessed with China. On more than one occasion, I've been shown around someone's garden and particular plants have been pointed out to me with comments such as "Of course, that's the Chinese form" or "The Chinese species is so much better, don't you think?" Now this is all very well, and I'd be the last to deny the huge contribution that China has made to our gardens. Unfortunately, enthusiastic credit to China has meant that credit to South America has too often been overlooked. South America is a big place and the fact that large swathes of it comprise tropical rain forest can fool you into believing that the only species of interest are those herbaceous types that can be grown as house plants or in heated conservatories. There are however huge parts of the South American continent with a temperate climate at least as cool as ours; and in the high Andes and the far south of course, a great deal that is very much colder.

The history of plant collection in South America began with the Spaniards who most famously brought us the potato in the sixteenth century and subsequently other plants of edible value, including the tomato (see pages 68-72). The collection of purely ornamental shrubs came some time later, in large measure because the Spanish weren't abundantly interested in them and were pretty keen, for all manner of reasons, to keep the British out of that continent. Among the few to 'escape' at that time was a shrub that I still grow and love and am saddened that it has

What shrubs do you recommend for autumn colour?

Because autumn has become synonymous with the changing colours of trees and because gardeners flock each year to the great national arboreta to see the displays, there has been a tendency to forget shrubs that provide autumn colour. And yet, in most gardens, you will obtain far better effect from a selection of shrubs than from the odd one or two trees for which you may have room. Here is a selection of some of my favourites:

Acer. Although almost all acers are really trees, some are small and others so slow growing that in many gardens they seldom reach more than shrub size. *A. palmatum dissectum* in its several forms is the most widely grown of these small forms and is a good species for autumn colour.

Berberis. Most berberis colour well, but the numerous forms of *B. thunbergii* are perhaps the best. Many varieties, such as 'Atropurpurea Nana', 'Dart's Purple' and 'Rose Glow' have purple foliage during the summer that later turns fiery red.

Ceratostigma willmottianum. The 'shrubby plumbago' is valuable for its late, clear-blue flowers and also for its foliage, which colours rich red in most years.

Cornus. Many of the dwarf dogwoods are valuable, but none more so than the varieties of *C. florida*.

Cotinus. Many gardeners think that the autumn colours of *C. coggygria* (the smoke bush) are unrivalled among shrubs. If its flowers cause 'smoke' in spring, its foliage certainly sets the autumn border alight.

Cotoneaster. Several cotoneasters have good autumn colour, but there are few reds more vivid than that of the much under-valued *C. horizontalis*.

Rhus. The stag's horn sumac undoubtedly produces a dramatic effect, seen against the autumn sun, but it then makes you pay for it with five months of looking like an undressed scarecrow.

Ribes. Some of the flowering currants produce good autumn foliage colour, the yellows and reds of *R. americanum* are perhaps best of all.

Roses. Shrub roses are excellent autumn plants. After their flowers have finished, they put on a superb display of hips if the birds allow and complement this with some glorious leaf colours. The yellows of the many varieties of *Rosa rugosa* are probably the most appealing.

Stephanandra. This is a valuable small genus of shrubs. Perhaps the most useful, not least for its autumn colour, is a none too vigorous, low-spreading plant, providing excellent ground cover, known as *S. incisa* 'Crispa'.

Viburnum. Another valuable genus and a large one, with many excellent deciduous and evergreen species. Two deciduous viburnums seen commonly and providing good autumn colours are *V. carlesii* and *V. opulus*.

been overshadowed by a Chinese relative. Until the end of the nineteenth century, the garden buddleja was the orange ball tree, *Buddleja globosa*, from Chile and Peru and introduced to Britain in 1774, but in modern gardens it has been usurped by the Oriental *Buddleja davidii*. With the gradual independence of the countries of South America in the nineteenth century, however, the wait for a real influx of shrubs came to an end; but my goodness, how worthwhile a wait it had been.

The Veitch nursery of Exeter was instrumental in giving the greatest impetus to shrub collection in South America when, in 1840 and then again in 1847, they sent two of their employees, the Cornish brothers William and Thomas Lobb, on collecting expeditions. The first journey took the two men through Argentina, into the Andes and most significantly into the cool forests of Chile. Later, they explored the south in greater detail, visiting Patagonia. Some of the plants that they found will be familiar to gardeners with rather closely defined conditions. *Embothrium coccineum*, the wonderful Chilean flame tree for instance, is at its best on acid soils in milder areas although the variety from the Longifolium Group from Tierra del Fuego is, not surprisingly, hardier. Eucryphias, also from Chile, are beautiful white-flowered shrubs or small trees, also for acidic soils but they will thrive in colder areas. *Eucryphia glutinosa* and *Eucryphia cordifolia* are both Chilean although, ironically, it wasn't until they were grown in an English garden that they hybridised to produce an even greater glory in *Eucryphia* x *nymansensis* 'Nymansay'.

Some of the best abutilons are South American. *Abutilon vitifolium*, a tall, perfectly hardy and elegant shrub with vine-like leaves, is another Chilean plant, introduced in 1837. But even more splendid, if slightly tender, is a Brazilian relative, *Abutilon megapotamicum*, a quite superb wall-shrub or climber with pendant red, yellow and black flowers. If you live in a cold area, grow it in your greenhouse or conservatory and be entranced. And grow also its Brazilian compatriot, *Abutilon pictum*, in the variegated form 'Thompsonii', the variegation intriguingly produced by virus contamination. But the virus doesn't pass from plant to plant other than in cuttings as it is naturally spread by a species of Brazilian whitefly that has been unable to find a home in Britain.

I have only scratched the surface of this subject and could equally have eulogised over the glorious evergreens, including *Crinodendron hookerianium* with its dark red lantern flowers or the holly-leaved *Desfontainea spinosa*. I've overlooked, too, the national flower of Chile, the incredibly sumptuous climber *Lapageria rosea*, a plant graced with the maiden name of the Empress Josephine. And even then, I would have omitted *Araucaria* species, the monkey puzzle tree and *Nothofagus* species, the southern beech, together with escallonias and fuchsias by the score.

Could you suggest two or three shrubs for a very shady spot?

There are still gardeners who consider shade a problem not an asset. I can only say that there are so many lovely plants positively demanding shade that if I didn't already have some shady places in my own garden, I would have to create them. Among shrubs, the list only becomes really short when the situation is not simply shaded but also very dry. My three suggestions nonetheless will be happy in almost any spot, even in fairly dense shade:

*Aucuba japonica (*Spotted laurel). Medium-sized evergreen with variously spotted leaves. Good varieties are 'Crotonifolia' with large yellowish leaf blotches and red berries, and 'Variegata' with masses of smaller yellow spots.

Daphne tangutica. Small, evergreen with small, elongated leaves and sweetly perfumed pink-purple flowers in early summer.

Sambucus nigra 'Aurea' (Golden elder). Deciduous, golden-foliage form of the common elder; 'Purpurea' is a dark purple-leaved variant.

ABOVE: *Had I been given the privilege of discovering one new plant in the wild, then it would have to have been the glorious South American evergreen* Berberis darwinii.

I have, however, saved one plant until the end. Charles Darwin saw it in Chile in 1835 but didn't collect it. That was left to William Lobb in 1848. *Berberis* is one of those genera that contains equally good and reliable deciduous and evergreen species but it includes one plant that has been called 'the finest evergreen ever to grace an English garden'. *Berberis darwinii* is named in memory of the greatest biologist of them all and no more fitting tribute could he have. Every time that I see it, bedecked in spring with its rich orange flowers, I feel that if ever I could have been privileged to discover a new plant growing in the wild, this would be it. We may be a long way from its South American homeland, but my goodness, how we have taken that plant to our gardening hearts. Yet I was appalled to discover recently that it had been deleted from the catalogue of one of our largest and finest shrub nurseries to make room for some modern invention belonging to the oriental *Berberis thunbergii*. Is nothing sacred?

The amazing leaf

I'VE OFTEN SAID that the most important colour in any garden is green. It's also the commonest and yet when we are planning and designing our gardens, it is the colour that we most take for granted. For green is by and large the colour of leaves, not of flowers, and it is therefore the colour that most plants have in common. And when I am asked about the importance of shapes in the garden, it's again to leaves that I turn first. Flowers and fruits are present for at most a few months of the year. Leaves are present for much longer. Deciduous plants have them for around seven months on average. Evergreen plants have leaves of some sort for 12 months; although contrary to what is often imagined, the same leaves aren't present permanently. Leaves drop from ever-

How effective are ground-cover shrubs at weed suppression?

Probably not as effective as some nurseries would have us believe. The ground-cover plant is one of the great *desiderata* of modern gardening offering, it is claimed, an easy and labour-saving way of covering a considerable area of soil.

What seems to have happened is that another modern requirement, the dwarf variety, has proved unable to compete with the full-sized weed and the ground-cover shrub has been invented to help it out. Unfortunately, ground-cover shrubs often fall short of expectations and there are very

greens just as they do from deciduous plants; they simply do it piecemeal.

Leaves should be appreciated for being probably the most significant and most interesting structures in the entire plant world. The green colour is caused by the presence of a chemical called chlorophyll that provides plants with the means to manufacture basic carbohydrate food substances from gases in the air. But leaves are also very important in a plant's uptake of water. Because water is lost through pores on the surface, more moisture is drawn up the plant from the roots.

The leaf is often a beautiful structure to look at but in its roles in photosynthesis and water regulation, it's also a beautiful example of the harnessing of form to function. A typical leaf represents a compromise between providing the maximum surface area for sunlight capture and yet minimising water loss to the point where it adequately helps to draw up water from below but doesn't deplete the plant of moisture more rapidly than the roots can balance with uptake from the soil. The compromise is dictated largely by the climate and conditions in which it grows. That this can sometimes fail is seen when large-leaved plants wilt in a dry soil in the height of summer and evergreens wilt in midwinter when the water in the soil is frozen.

Although most leaves are divided into a stalk (even if this is rudimentary) and a more or less flattened part called the blade, the variation in overall leaf size and form among plants is enormous. And it's just this variation that is so important in garden design. The simplest leaf form has the overall appearance of a spearhead but from this basic type, variations occur that encompass all manner of intricate and complex indentations, lobes and teeth. Many leaves are subdivided into separate leaflets in a range of different ways but almost all of these shapes are basic adaptations that serve the dual

few among them that fulfil all of the hoped-for criteria. The weeds will still grow while the infant slow-growing plant takes many years to reach maturity. Hand-weeding must take over, but hand-weeding among ground cover, especially prickly ground cover like low-growing roses, can be a nightmare. By contrast, the faster establishing and maturing ground-cover species are quite likely to subjugate, along with the weeds, the other garden plants whose well-being they are intended to aid. Ultimately, many plants so widely recommended as ground cover (and the infamous Rose of Sharon, *Hypericum calycinum*, must top this list) will, in most modern gardens, become a greater menace than any annual weeds and, even then, present little threat to many of the most troublesome perennials. Ground-cover plants can be very attractive but they don't offer the ultimate answer to weed control.

purposes of light capture and water regulation in different habitats.

The appearance of leaves tells us more than any other feature about the conditions that any particular plant is likely to require in the garden. For instance, the highly indented leaf of a woodland fern provides a large surface area for light capture in a poorly lit environment, while its smooth surface and overall thinness which would encourage water loss, indicate that it prefers a moist atmosphere where such water loss would cause no problem. So if you plant a fern in hot sunshine, the fragile leaf tissues will almost certainly scorch and the plant suffer as its photosynthesising tissues

are inevitably dried out. Conversely, the reason that so many alpine plants are difficult to grow in gardens is because they have densely hairy leaves, adapted to minimise water loss in the drying mountain-top conditions of high sunlight and strong winds. Those same hairy leaves in a lowland garden will trap moisture and encourage the setting in of fungal decay.

But it's in the autumn that leaves take on their greatest importance in gardens. The leaves of many deciduous trees then draw attention to themselves by changing colour dramatically. Greens disappear to reveal yellows, reds and oranges, as individual leaves reach the end of their lives and become increasingly moribund. Chlorophyll production slowly ceases, and so exposes other coloured pigments, especially yellow carotenoids. Sometimes other pigments such as red anthocyanins are produced at the same time, so enhancing further the remarkably attractive appearance of autumn foliage. At least some of these processes are brought about by changes in temperature as well as the length of daylight, and this is the reason why some maples develop better colour in North America than they do in Britain (see pages 139-141). So, even in their death throes, leaves can be among the most beautiful things in your garden.

Native trees and shrubs for the garden hedgerow

MANY AN ENGLISHMAN travelling abroad has hankered for the fields and woods of his homeland. And many a traveller returning has commented on the beauty of the tree-adorned British countryside. We may not have as dense a tree and shrub cover as historically we did, nor as many species as some other parts of the world. We do, however, still have a diverse, rich and beautiful flora of woody plants. And whilst to my mind a grouping of native plants cannot by itself create a garden, I do believe that every garden, big or small, should have a small collection. Not only does this encourage us to appreciate our own plants the better, it also provides a valuable habitat for native wildlife.

Unless your garden is truly big, you should avoid making the mistake of planting large tree species; they will soon dwarf the garden and cause you headaches instead of pleasure. As full-sized individuals, they are for the forest. But hedgerows offer a wonderful opportunity to grow big plants to manageable size. Hedges, of course, aren't natural. In reality, few things are more artificial and in simple terms a hedge is no more than a long, narrow wood, rather strictly managed. But I can usefully differentiate between garden hedges and traditional or farm hedges. The differences lie in their age and in the range and types of species they contain. The garden hedge usually includes one species only and has been planted fairly recently; the 'traditional' hedge is generally much older and much more diverse, the two things often being directly related, as I shall come to in a moment.

Which are the best buys among dwarf conifers?

There has been a phenomenal growth of interest in dwarf conifers in the past few decades, and nurseries specialising in these plants may offer more than a thousand different varieties. The plants that I have chosen are all fairly easily obtained, but a visit to a specialist supplier will reveal the real potential that dwarf conifers offer.

Even traditional hedges, however, were originally planted with only one tree or shrub species, but others often colonise naturally as seeds are blown in or carried by birds or animals. The total number of plant species recorded in British hedgerows is very large, and as many as 300 occur quite frequently; to the extent that the English names of some plants have hedge as a prefix; hedge garlic (*Alliaria petiolata*) and hedge mustard (*Sisymbrium officinale*), for instance. Whilst there are some very marked regional variations in the woody species composition of hedgerows, reflecting climatic or historical factors (fuchsias are common in the south west of Britain and beech is used extensively around Exmoor, for instance), there are also clear national trends. The commonest tree species are oak (*Quercus robur* and *Quercus petraea*), ash (*Fraxinus excelsior*), beech (*Fagus sylvatica*) and sycamore (*Acer pseudoplatanus*). Elm, which of course used to be of such major importance, has diminished dramatically or almost vanished over the past 25 years as a result of Dutch elm disease.

Sometimes, the trees of hedgerows are the result of individual specimens of the planted hedgerow species having been allowed to grow to maturity; sometimes they have been planted in addition to the main hedgerow species or, very

FIRS. *Abies koreana, A. nordmanniana* 'Golden Spreader'.

CEDARS. *Cedrus deodara* 'Golden Horizon'.

CYPRESSES. *Chamaecyparis lawsoniana* 'Ellwood's Pillar', *C. lawsoniana* 'Minima Aurea'.

JUNIPERS. *J. horizontalis* 'Emerald Spreader', *J. x media* 'Old Gold', *J. squamata* 'Blue Carpet'

SPRUCES. *Picea glauca* 'Albertiana Conica'.

PINES. *Pinus strobus* 'Nana'.

YEWS. *Taxus baccata* 'Standishii'.

RED CEDARS. *Thuja orientalis* 'Aurea Nana'.

frequently, they have colonised naturally and been allowed to grow to maturity by the farmer sparing the cutters. The plant used most commonly for traditional hedgerow planting is hawthorn (*Crataegus laevigata* or *Crataegus monogyna*). Most other shrubs that now occur so commonly in hedgerows are natural colonisers; such plants as wild privet (*Ligustrum vulgare*, not the same as the garden privet which is an introduced Japanese species), dog rose (*Rosa canina*), spindle (*Euonymus europaeus*) or elderberry (*Sambucus nigra*) are most unlikely to have been planted as farm boundaries as they are not robust enough to contain livestock.

As a result of extensive surveys of the species composition of hedgerows and careful study of old maps and recorded planting dates, it's been possible to devise a system for estimating the age of hedges. Given a number of qualifications, such as the need for several samples, the need to avoid lengths of hedge that adjoin woods or gardens (where, clearly, deliberate planting is a major influence), a rough rule of thumb is that, within a 30m run of hedgerow, the number of species of tree or shrub, counted from one side, indicates the age of the hedge in hundreds of years. I have found, moreover, that this system can be useful for old garden hedges. I have a length of boundary hedge containing hawthorn, yew, ash, holly (*Ilex aquifolium*), wild gooseberry (*Ribes uva-crispa*), bramble (*Rubus fructicosus*) and blackthorn (*Prunus spinosa*). Whilst I don't pretend that this gives me a precise date for my hedgerow, I think that the large number of wild species means it is safe to assume that it is probably the original boundary of the property (the house is approximately 350 years old) or even an earlier field hedge incorporated into the boundary.

I hope that I have encouraged you to plant a replica of a traditional hedge, or at least, a short length of it in your own garden. Not only will you create something of year-round appeal and beauty, you will also attract a very wide range of animal and bird life to enrich your garden environment.

INDEX

PICTURE CREDITS

Professor Stefan Buczacki: 14-15, 27, 90
Jerry Harpur: 102, 130, 131
The Garden Picture Library: 38-9, 83,
GPL/John Bethell 34-5, GPL/Lynne
Brotchie 119, 122-3, GPL/Guy Bouchet
43, GPL/Brian Carter 154-5,
GPL/John Glover 67, GPL/Vaughan

Fleming 71, GPL/Sunniva Harte 127,
GPL/Gary Rogers 158-9, GPL/JS Sira
46-47, GPL/Ron Sutherland 10-11,
18-19, 30-31, GPL/Brigitte Thomas 23,
146-7, GPL/Steven Wooster 110-111
Clive Nichols Garden Pictures: 2-3, 3, 42,
79, 94-5, 107

Neil Campbell-Sharpe: 51, 62-3, 74-5,
91, 99, 103, 106, 114-5, 122, 126, 134-5,
138, 142, 150
Elizabeth Whiting Associates: 15, 26-7,
54-5, 59, 70, 86-7, 139